# CELEBRATING LEICESTER

STEPHEN BUTT

First published 2021

Amberley Publishing, The Hill, Stroud
Gloucestershire GL5 4EP

www.amberley-books.com

Copyright © Stephen Butt, 2021

The right of Stephen Butt to be identified as the Author of this work has been asserted in accordance with the Copyrights, Designs and Patents Act 1988.

All rights reserved. No part of this book may be reprinted or reproduced or utilised in any form or by any electronic, mechanical or other means, now known or hereafter invented, including photocopying and recording, or in any information storage or retrieval system, without the permission in writing from the Publishers.

British Library Cataloguing in Publication Data.
A catalogue record for this book is available from the British Library.

ISBN 978 1 3981 0654 3 (print)
ISBN 978 1 3981 0655 0 (ebook)

Typesetting by SJmagic DESIGN SERVICES, India.
Printed in Great Britain.

# Contents

Introduction   4

1. Celebrating People   8
2. Invented in Leicester   26
3. Leicester Makes It Worldwide   35
4. Institutions, Charities and Sport   51
5. Buildings and Special Places   65
6. Traditions   81
7. Music, Arts, and the Media   88

# Introduction

We feel better when we celebrate. We all enjoy hearing good news. Whether it is a personal or family achievement, a spectacular win by our football team or a breakthrough in medicine, it makes us feel good, and it brings us together, as families, teams, workmates, and colleagues.

The coronavirus pandemic of 2020 affected the physical and mental health of millions of people across the world with tragic consequences for many. Leicester's

Leicester's ever-changing skyline. This view, taken in 2005, is looking south from Charles Street.

lockdown was extended because of the high infection rate. There have been other times of crisis in the city's long history, but there has also been much to celebrate. Behind each achievement, idea, invention and work of art there has been a person who has made life better in some way for others, from pneumatic tyres, potato crisps and glacier mints to space travel and DNA fingerprinting.

Clocks built by Gents of Leicester were marking the time in hospitals, factories and schools across the country. Hundreds of thousands of clerks and secretaries used typewriters made by Imperial Typewriters. Schoolchildren learned how to work with a multitude of crafts using Dryad products from Leicester.

Nicola Pellow wrote the computer code for the first ever web browser when a student in Leicester. Perin Towlson, a De Montfort University graduate, designed and made the porcelain caskets containing the soil from where Richard III was born, raised and died, for his re-interment. Louis de Bernieres, author of *Captain Corelli's Mandolin*, also studied at De Montfort University when it was Leicester Polytechnic.

Most towns and cities have similar success stories, but perhaps Leicester is different because of its industrial diversity. Whereas some cities are known for one major industry or significant individual, Leicester is a city of many different elements. Indeed, it has been described as a city full of surprises.

Leicester's prosperity over the past two centuries was due largely to its mighty textile and footwear industries which created the need for many other technologies

Abbey Park opened in 1882, but its history dates back to the eleventh century with the founding of the abbey by Robert de Beaumont, 2nd Earl of Leicester.

and support businesses. At the height of its post-war prosperity, Leicester was exporting shoe machinery across the world and its famous shoe brands were in almost every High Street in the country. From the shoe industry grew the rubber industry, manufacturing car and bicycle tyres.

Three-quarters of all cinemagoers watched films projected through lenses made in in the city. Garments made in Leicester were sold by major chain stores including Marks and Spencer, British Home Stores and Littlewoods.

It could not last. Leicester's largest industries lacked sufficient investment after the Second World War and were then hit by the first great wave of globalisation and competing cheaper imports that flooded into Britain. Eventually, Leicester diversified. Today, many of the old factories are home to new service industries and technologies. The city is a major logistics base for the movement of raw materials and goods, and it is now looking even further afield, to the planets and the stars.

Leicester's recorded history stretches back to before the Romans reached the area in AD 48. It still has a rich heritage of buildings which are noble, fascinating, and delightful to view. It has centuries of traditions, and an impressive roll call of men and women who have gained recognition for their contributions to society.

I must record my gratitude to all those Leicester folk who have contributed to this book. These include Dr Liam McCarthy, Patrick Hostler, Perin Towlson and many others. No research can be the product of just one individual. I have referred to many historical texts and discussed thoughts with local people who know their city well. I happily acknowledge their contributions and guidance.

*Left*: Olympic champion Jennie Fletcher, who held England and World swimming records in the early twentieth century.

*Opposite above*: Dating to the eleventh century, Leicester Castle has played a central role in the history of the city, hosting royal visits, parliamentary gatherings and law courts.

*Opposite below*: The Cinema de Lux and John Lewis department store façade at the Highcross Centre, designed by the architectural team of Farshid Moussavi OBE, RA and Alejandro Zaera-Polo.

# Celebrating People

The people of Leicester have been prominent on the world stage for centuries. There have been missionaries, anthropologists, explorers of the Amazon, scientists and footballers, Olympic swimmers, machine tool manufacturers, water engineers, politicians, novelists, film directors, furniture designers, makers of confectionery and organisers of comedy festivals.

The work of an undergraduate at Leicester Polytechnic enabled the world to use the internet. Having enrolled on a mathematics sandwich course, Nicola Pellow was attached to the headquarters of CERN, the European Council for Nuclear Research, working under Tim Berners-Lee. As a member of the small team that

Nicola Pellow, who wrote the first-ever internet browser, with Tim Berners-Lee, photographed in the 1990s.

created the World Wide Web, Nicola wrote the machine code for the first-ever web browser to work on any computer. Her work made the internet accessible to everyone for the first time.

There are two brothers the sons of Frank Attenborough, second Principal of the University of Leicester who, although not born in Leicester, most certainly belong to the city. A presence for many decades on stage and screen, Lord Richard Attenborough's first acting appearance was at Leicester's Little Theatre. He studied at Wyggeston Boys' School and then attended RADA. In his long and distinguished career, he acted in or directed nearly eighty films and gained numerous honours and awards. His first film role was in *In Which We Serve* in 1942, playing the un-credited role of a deserting soldier. In real life, he served with the RAF, undergoing pilot training, and was then seconded to the RAF film unit at Pinewood Studios.

Lord Attenborough supported many charitable activities worldwide but remained close to the city. In 2007, he and Lady Attenborough entrusted their collection of Picasso ceramics to Leicester in memory of their daughter, Jane, and granddaughter, Lucy, who had both perished in the Asian Tsunami

The New Walk Museum. A place of inspiration and exploration since it opened in 1849 as one of the first public museums in the UK.

on 26 December 2004. A permanent exhibition of items from the collection is housed at the Art Gallery in New Walk. Lord Attenborough was also the driving force behind *Embrace Arts*, formerly the Richard Attenborough Centre for Disability and the Arts in Leicester.

The story by Michael Crichton for the film *Jurassic Park* in which Lord Attenborough played John Hammond, who opens a wildlife park containing cloned dinosaurs, could not have been written before Sir Alec Jeffries developed the techniques of genetic fingerprinting and DNA profiling at Leicester University, coincidentally the academic institution where Frederick Attenborough was principal when it was a University College.

Sir David Attenborough is one of the world's most well-known and respected naturalists and authorities on conservation. His childhood was spent in and around College House on the campus of the University of Leicester. He too attended Wyggeston Boys' School before gaining his first degree from Clare College, Cambridge.

In 1950, Sir David joined the BBC and by 1969 had become Director of Programmes for the two main BBC Television channels. His name was proposed as a future Director General, but he resigned to concentrate on his true passion of programme-making. He has been called 'the great communicator', 'the peerless educator' and 'the greatest broadcaster of our time'. Underlying his lifetime's achievements is his boyish fascination for wildlife which began in Leicester with visits to the New Walk Museum.

*Above left and above right*: Fellow explorers and adventurers from Leicester: Alfred Russel Wallace (seated) and Henry Bates.

A name familiar to the young David Attenborough when he was exploring the exhibits of the New Walk Museum is that of Alfred Russel Wallace, who for a time taught at the nearby Collegiate School. Wallace became the leading expert of his generation on the geographic distribution of animal species. A respected evolutionary theorist, he was co-discoverer with Charles Darwin of the theory of natural selection. He was also one of the first scientists to write a serious paper on whether there was life on Mars. Several hundred species of plants and animals, living and in fossil form, have been named after Wallace as well as craters on Mars and the moon.

At Leicester's Town Library, Wallace met Henry Bates, who was to become a close friend and colleague. They collaborated on a 'great adventure' in the Amazon Rainforest and in April 1848 left for Pará, now Belém, near the mouth of the Amazon.

Wallace returned to England in 1852 after his ship caught fire and sank. Bates stayed in Brazil for a further eleven years, discovering what is now called Batesian mimicry, which describes how some harmless butterflies became adapted to mimic the colouration of poisonous members of their species so were less likely to be eaten by birds which had learned to avoid the poisonous ones.

It took Bates three years to write up his research in a paper titled *The Naturalist on the River Amazon*. It is still regarded as one of the finest natural history reports of any time.

More recently, a figure from history who sought and fought for fame during his lifetime became infinitely more well-known after over 500 years when his remains were uncovered under a Leicester car park. The discovery and identification of Richard III in 2012 has been described as one of the top ten archaeological discoveries of the decade worldwide.

The king's remains were found during an archaeological dig at the site of the former Grey Friars, led by Mathew Morris of ULAS, the University of Leicester Archaeological Studies. The success of the project and the identification of Richard III was the result of the combined expertise of many academics at Leicester University in the fields of archaeology, genetics, osteology, and genealogy. They worked with other organisations including the Richard III Society and Leicester City Council. The king's remains were reburied at Leicester Cathedral in 2015.

Perin Towlson is a ceramicist working in Leicester as a studio potter and artist. She graduated from De Montfort University in 2011 with an honours degree in Design Crafts. She was commissioned to create two sets of three porcelain-lidded boxes to contain the blessed soil from where Richard III was born (Fotheringhay Castle), lived (Middleham Castle) and died (Fenn Lane, Bosworth in Leicestershire). One set is on display at the Bosworth Battlefield Heritage Visitor Centre. The other set is at Leicester Cathedral.

The award-winning feature film *The Elephant Man*, released in 1980, directed by David Lynch and starring John Hurt in the title role, brought the life of Leicester's Joseph Carey Merrick to worldwide attention. There was tragedy in

*Left*: The Richard III statue was donated to Leicester by the Richard III Society in 1980. It was later relocated from Castle Gardens to the cathedral precincts near to where the king's remains were discovered.

*Below*: Early mobile marketing by Thomas Cook & Sons Ltd. The event advertised is an illustrated lantern slide lecture at Kibworth Village Hall.

Thomas Cook's worldwide travel business began with a railway excursion from Leicester. Later, the company offered holidays by rail across Great Britain and beyond.

his life in the latter half of the eighteenth century because of his obvious physical disabilities and the harsh treatment he received at the hands of his father and stepmother, but research has shown Joseph to have been a brave and principled man, admired, not shunned, by those who knew him. He gained many friends who cared for him and respected him.

Fighting to improve the conditions of working-class families such as the Merricks, the young preacher Thomas Cook became convinced that temperance was the answer to many of the social problems of the time. He, like Joseph Merrick's mother, was a Baptist.

Cook was born in Melbourne in Derbyshire, and after working as a travelling missionary across several counties in the East Midlands he settled in Market Harborough. While travelling from his home to attend a temperance rally in Leicester, he had his idea of using the developing railway system to help social reform. Cook suggested that a special train could be hired to take temperance supporters to a forthcoming meeting in Loughborough. He contacted the Midland Railway Company, and on 5 July 1841 nearly 500 people took the journey from Leicester's Campbell Street station to Loughborough and back.

The event was successful in social terms, and financially because Cook made a profit. He later commented, 'Thus was struck the keynote of my excursions, and the social idea grew upon me.'

He arranged many similar excursions, providing thousands of workers in the towns of the Midlands with their first experience of railway travel and an environment away from the lure of alcohol. Setting the standards for his future business success, Cook planned each aspect of the project, travelling the routes

Thomas Cook saw the potential in integrating public transport to take people from their own towns direct to faraway places.

Thomas Cook was a philanthropist motivated principally by his religious faith. It was his son, John Mason Cook, who took the business forward and created the worldwide brand.

beforehand and writing a handbook for passengers to read during the journey. His careful attention to detail, effective advertising and the low cost of tickets created a tourism business of international renown.

Cook's priority was his desire to encourage social reform. The sustained success of his company was due to the business and management prowess of his son, John Mason Cook. Sadly, the company ceased trading in 2019, but a great social legacy remains. The company Cook founded provided millions of people with the holiday of a lifetime. The company's substantial archive is now held at the Record Office for Leicestershire, Leicester and Rutland.

Another member of the Baptist movement to settle in Leicester was William Carey. From a shoemaking family in Northamptonshire, Carey became the minister of the Harvey Lane Chapel in 1789. Four years later, he and his family travelled to India to become the first Baptist missionary and founder of the Baptist Missionary Society. When he died, in India in 1834, translations of the Bible had been made available in forty languages.

The Harvey Lane chapel was destroyed by fire in 1921. Its replacement was demolished in 1963 and Carey's former cottage was also demolished in 1968 to make way for the city's inner ring road. The Holiday Inn now stands on the site. A small collection of items from Carey's life and work are kept on display at the Central Baptist Church in Charles Street.

*Above*: The interior of William Carey's cottage after the building and contents were converted into a museum.

*Left*: The opening of William Carey's cottage as a museum. The crowds and men looking out of first-floor windows indicate Carey's significance to Baptists in Leicester.

Many historians have recorded the events of the past and written about the people who shaped Leicester. They all owe a debt to John Nichols who published his massive *History and Antiquities of the County of Leicester* in eight great volumes between 1795 and 1815. Despite errors and inconsistencies, Nichols' work is still the starting point for any research into Leicester and its county.

*Right*: A portrait of antiquarian historian John Nichols by John Baptist Jackson, engraved by Charles Heath.

*Below*: John Nichols' History & Antiquities of the County of Leicester (1795–1815) was published in eight large volumes containing 5.5 million words. This is a volume from the 1971 reprint.

Thomas White never lived in Leicester and probably never visited the town, but his benevolence fostered the birth and growth of thousands of small businesses throughout the area. His image stands with those of Simon de Montfort, William Wyggeston and Alderman Newton flanking Leicester's clock tower.

In the sixteenth century, he set up a charity to support young men who wanted to enter the world of business and commerce. It was a path he had trod with great success. As an ambitious young man, White was managing his own business before the age of thirty and rose rapidly to become Lord Mayor of London in 1546. He was also the founder of St John's College, Oxford.

White was a man of great generosity. Although he lived comfortably, he had few possessions and little money at the time of his death, having given most of it away. An indication of the wealth he amassed is the value of his foundation, which in 2012 had reserves of over £3.5million. It is still providing interest-free loans to fledgling businesses.

Gary Winston Lineker is a footballer of world renown, not least because of his career record of never having committed a foul or having been presented with a yellow or red card. His father, grandfather and great-grandfather were

The laying of the foundations of Leicester's clock tower in 1868. One of the men is the stonemason who created the four statues, of William Wyggeston, Thomas White, Gabriel Newton and Simon de Montfort, which surround the tower.

greengrocers, and the family still trades on Leicester's market. He went to Caldecote Road School and Leicester Boys' Grammar School. As a boy, he excelled in cricket and football. From the age of eleven he captained the Leicestershire Schools cricket team and believed he had more chance of succeeding at cricket than football. When he left school with four basic O levels, one teacher commented that he 'concentrates too much on football' and that he would 'never make a living at that'. Shortly afterwards he joined the youth academy at Leicester City.

His career is legendary. Lineker retired from international football with eighty caps and forty-eight goals. He transferred to a new career in television. His popularity enabled him to feature in commercials for Leicester-based Walkers Crisps, who temporarily named their salt and vinegar crisps 'Salt-n-Lineker'. In 2016 when Leicester City won the Premiership title, he was possibly upstaged by top goal-scorer Jamie Vardy, whose image promoted a limited edition of 'Vardy Salted' crisps.

Dion Dublin was born in Leicester in 1969. He played for several Leicestershire youth teams including Wigston Fields and Thurmaston Magpies and began his professional footballing career with Norwich City after leaving school in 1985. He made his name at Cambridge United as a centre-forward.

He is also an amateur percussionist, and invented an instrument called 'The Dube'. He has accompanied the Birmingham rock band *Ocean Colour Scene* in a gig at the University of East Anglia. He has also worked as a commentator for Sky Sports and on BBC Radio 5 Live's *Fighting Talk*.

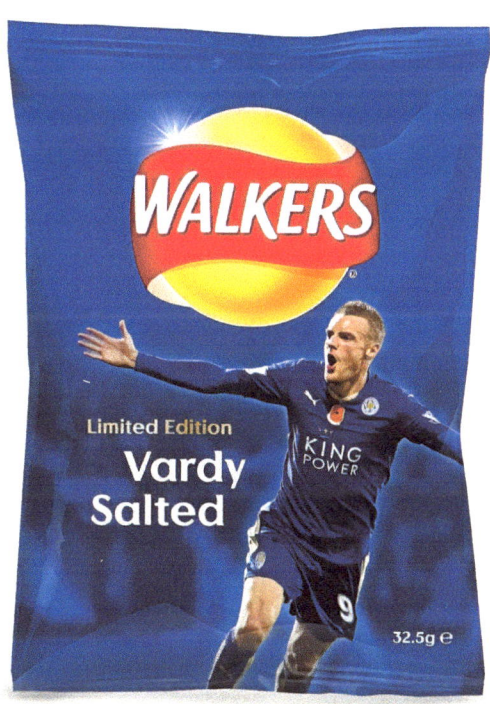

After 'Salt and Lineker' crisps came this renamed snack from Walkers Crisps to celebrate Leicester City's premiership title win in 2016.

Dion Dublin has no doubt encountered arts and crafts furniture as a presenter of the BBC One daytime show *Homes Under the Hammer*, and arguably the greatest designer of that genre was Ernest Gimson of Leicester.

Gimson was born in in 1864, the son of iron founder Josiah Gimson. He was articled to the Leicester architect Isaac Barradale, and worked at his offices on Grey Friars.

His career was defined when, in 1883, he attended a lecture on 'Art and Socialism' at the Leicester Secular Society in Humberstone Gate given by William Morris, the leader of the Arts and Crafts revival. Greatly inspired, Gimson talked with Morris after the lecture until 2.00 a.m.

Two years later, Gimson had gained a first-class result from the Leicester School of Art. He moved to London with letters of recommendation from Morris. He was taken on by John Dando Sedding, whose offices were next door to the showrooms of the Morris company.

After travelling in Britain and Europe, Gimson settled in London and joined Morris's Society for the Protection of Ancient Buildings. Through the Art Workers' Guild, he became interested in a more 'hands-on' approach to traditional crafts. He learned to make rush-seated ladderback chairs and experimented with plaster work.

Today his furniture and craft work are regarded as a supreme achievement of the period and a lasting influence on interior design.

The Leicester Secular Hall. Ernest Gimson was inspired to follow a career in architecture and design by a talk given here by Arts & Crafts pioneer William Morris.

John Breedon Everard. A notable architect, but principally a construction engineer who worked on projects including railways and reservoirs.

The son of a mine and quarry owner, John Breedon Everard was an influential civil engineer and architect, and co-founder of the firm Pick Everard. In 1866 he became assistant resident engineer for the construction of the final section of the Midland Railway route into London from Kentish Town to St Pancras. This involved several complex engineering challenges including viaducts and tunnels. Two years later he set up in practice as a civil engineer in Leicester.

He became a partner in his father's firm, Ellis & Everard, and was involved in the development of the Bardon Hill quarry, which included designing a school and two churches.

Numerous appointments followed in disciplines including geology, engineering, mining and architecture. He was elected a fellow of the Geological Society in 1870, a member of the Institution of Civil Engineers in 1886, and a fellow of the Royal Institute of British Architects in 1887.

He also specialised in water supply projects. He helped initiate the Derwent Valley scheme to supply water to Leicester, Nottingham, Sheffield and Derby, taking responsibility for the Leicester section of the scheme from Sawley to Hallgates, which included an aqueduct across the River Trent. His work also included the buildings at Swithland Reservoir, completed in 1896.

Everard designed a Turkish bath in Leicester's Friar Lane, the Tower Brewery in Southgate Street for his uncle, William Everard, and the Leicestershire

George Hostler. A sculptor who later turned knitted jumpers into fashion statements for celebrities.

South African War Memorial in Town Hall Square. He was High Sheriff of Leicestershire in 1913.

Rosemary Conley CBE was born in Leicester in 1946. She attended Bushloe High School in Leicestershire and Goddard's Secretarial College in Leicester and studied for a Royal Society of Arts qualification in Exercise to Music. After losing weight herself, Conley began evening classes for local women under the name of the *Slimming & Good Grooming Club*.

Rosemary chose a low-fat diet as an alternative to surgery for gallstones. This inspired her to sell the diet to others as *The Hip & Thigh Diet* in 1988, which sold over two million copies. In 1996, the Rosemary Conley Diet and Fitness magazine was launched, which became the market leader in its sector after only three issues. From 1996 to 2000 she was a consultant to Marks and Spencer, helping to develop their low-fat, calorie-controlled food range.

From 1993 to 2014 she was the founder and president of Rosemary Conley Diet and Fitness Clubs and later, chairman of Digital Wellbeing Ltd, the parent company of Rosemary Online. She was appointed deputy lieutenant of Leicestershire in 1991 and in 2001 became the first woman to be granted the Freedom of the City of Leicester.

George Hostler, who died in 2018, helped turn knitted jumpers into fashion statements. He graduated with a fine arts degree from Durham University to become a successful sculptor with an international reputation. He turned to textiles and was appointed Head of the Design Foundation Department at Leicester Polytechnic. Setting up his own design house, he created knitwear for Zandra Rhodes and Stirling Cooper, made jumpers for Elton John, Diana, Princess of Wales, actors John Inman, Richard Briers and Bonnie Langford, and sold through Harrods in London and Bloomingdales in New York.

Mary Ellen 'Nellie' Taylor, the daughter of Leicester businessman and inventor Thomas Taylor, had the dubious honour of being the subject of one of the first police surveillance photographs in England. On 5 March 1910, she organised a Women's Social and Political Union (WSPU) meeting in Kibworth Village Hall where a mainly female audience heard speeches by suffragettes Alice Pemberton-Peake and Dorothy Pethick. On the day before this meeting Nellie Taylor was praised by *Votes for Women*, a newspaper dedicated to the suffragettes' cause.

In 1911 Nellie and her daughter Lily Dorothea boycotted the census, her husband Tom writing 'No Vote No Census' on their forms. It is possible that they spent the day at a boycott party at the WSPU shop in Bowling Green Lane in Leicester with other suffragettes. Nellie's sister, Elizabeth, organised one such party in Hackney.

By early 1912 Nellie was a highly active member of the WSPU, the leading militant organisation campaigning for Women's suffrage, and on 4 March 1912, took part in a window-smashing incident at a post office in London's Sloane Square.

Those involved were arrested and appeared before a magistrate at Westminster Police Court. The case was referred to the Sessions and their application for bail was refused. They were remanded in custody to Holloway Prison. The punishment was more severe than expected. Nellie Taylor was sentenced to three months' imprisonment.

Leicester, with its tradition of supporting minority voices and opinions, was generally supportive of the suffragette movement.

Alice Hawkins was probably its most dynamic member locally. She was a mother of six children and worked as a machinist at Equity Shoes. In 1896 she joined the factory's Women's Co-operative Guild, having been a member of the Independent Labour Party since 1894.

Alice was arrested five times and committed to Holloway Prison, but her voice was not silenced. In 1913 she spoke at a meeting with David Lloyd George and Sir Edward Grey. With others, she explained the poor pay and working conditions suffered by women and their hope that a vote would empower women to challenge these inequalities. Hawkins explained how her fellow male workers could choose a man to represent them whilst the women were left unrepresented.

Her protests ended in the following year with the outbreak of the First World War. The WSPU agreed to stop their protests if all prisoners from the movement were released. 1,300 women had been arrested over the year for supporting the cause as well as more than 100 men including Alice Hawkins' husband Alfred.

Equity Shoes, a pioneering workers co-operative, was the last major shoe manufacturer in Leicestershire. It closed in 2009.

One of the most tenacious members of the Suffragette movement was Lillian Lenton who was born in Leicester in 1891. She trained as a dancer, but, after hearing Emmeline Pankhurst speak, decide to join the WPSU as soon as she was old enough. In March 1912, with other members, she took part in a window-smashing campaign. She was imprisoned for two months.

In 1913, she began a series of arson attacks in London, and was arrested on suspicion of setting fire to the Tea House at Kew Gardens. In Holloway Prison she held a hunger strike for two days before being forcibly fed, which caused her to become seriously ill with pleurisy caused by food entering her lungs. Her case created an outrage among the public. To avoid more such political embarrassment, the government rushed through its 'Cat and Mouse Act', which stated that hunger-striking suffragette 'mice' could be released on temporary licence to recover their health, when the security forces could re-arrest them.

In June 1913 Lillie was arrested in Doncaster and charged with being on the premises of an unoccupied house which had been set on fire. She was released from Armley Prison in Leeds after several days. Later, to avoid re-capture for further offences, she was smuggled out of the country to France by friends.

She was arrested on numerous occasions and frequently went on hunger strike. Because of the frequency of her escapes Lenton became known as the 'tiny, wily, elusive Pimpernel'. She received a Hunger Strike Medal 'for Valour' from the WSPU.

During the First World War, she served in Serbia with the Scottish Women's Hospitals Unit and was awarded a French Red Cross medal. She later worked in the British Embassy in Stockholm and was a speaker for the Save the Children Fund. From 1924 for ten years she was a travel organiser for the Women's Freedom League and editor of the League's Bulletin. After working in Scotland in animal welfare, Lillie became the financial secretary of the National Union of Women Teachers until 1953.

In 1970, as Treasurer of the Suffragette Fellowship, she unveiled a memorial in Christchurch Gardens, Westminster, dedicated to all the women who had fought to get the vote. Lillie Lenton died in 1972.

Jennie Fletcher's family owned a fish shop in the Belgrave area. Born in 1890, she attended Mellor Road Primary School, but as one of eleven children, out of necessity she worked in a textile factory from a young age and could only focus on her favourite pastime of swimming after working a twelve-hour shift for six days a week.

In the first decade of the twentieth century Jennie became Britain's leading female amateur swimmer, breaking numerous records. In 1906 she was Leicester's all-round swimming champion. Two thousand people saw her become the English 100 yards Swimming Champion at a competition in her local Cossington Street baths. She remained an amateur, winning six ASA 100 yards freestyle titles between 1906 and 1912, and setting a world record for the distance in 1909. In all she won twenty major titles and set eleven world records.

Jennie became a household name, attracting large crowds and swimming for the UK in the 1912 Summer Olympics in Stockholm where she won bronze in the 100 metres freestyle and gold in the 4 x 100 metre relay. She and her teammates competed in expensive silk swimming costumes. The lightweight and body-revealing costumes were designed on scientific principles but were regarded by some as immodest.

Jennie retired from swimming in 1913. She and her husband, Henry Hyslop, emigrated to Canada where they had a daughter and five sons. She became a member of the International Swimming Hall of Fame in Florida in 1971 and died in 1968. Her daughter Betty recalls that her mother always spoke modestly about her career: 'She was so modest and if her career was discussed, she'd say, "Oh, that was a long time ago and I did it because I just loved to swim."'

# Invented in Leicester

A collision at a railway crossing near Markfield in Leicestershire led to the invention of a steam-powered whistle which could be attached to railway locomotives. No one was injured when the locomotive hit a cart carrying eggs and butter to Leicester market, but the accident was serious enough for the railway pioneer Robert Stephenson to intervene.

Stephenson went to a musical instrument maker in Duke Street in Leicester who made a 'steam trumpet' which was tried out in the presence of the railway company's directors. It was attached to *Samson*, the locomotive involved in the accident, and fed with dry steam from the engine's boiler. The company later attached whistles to all its locomotives.

Britain's first traffic wardens were recruited and trained in Leicester. They were based at the City Police headquarters in Charles Street.

Traffic management of a different kind was invented in Leicester. The role of traffic warden was created in the city in April 1961 by the then Chief Constable, Sir Robert Mark.

It is probably apocryphal that Sir Robert's initiative was prompted by John Fortune, the editor of the *Leicester Mercury*, who complained that traffic congestion near the clock tower delayed his newspaper vans delivering the latest editions to street vendors.

Walkie-talkies were not invented in Leicester, but the man who invented them was born in the city. Donald Lewes Hing emigrated with his family to Canada and became a pioneer in telecommunications. He is best known for his invention of the walkie-talkie used during the Second World War. His grandson, Morgan Burke, remembered, 'Having a gifted inventor as a grandfather was [...] well, it was perfectly normal if that was the only grandfather you knew. He did all the things that I thought grandfathers were supposed to do, like build Morse code toys out of cigar boxes and nine-volt batteries, and run antennas out of your bedroom window and up a tree in the backyard, so that your home-made short-wave set could pick up the Tokyo time signal.'

In 1946, Hing was awarded the MBE. His life's work included a vast range of radio technologies and geophysical exploration techniques using electromagnetic instrumentation. He took out more than fifty patents in Canada

Donald Hings. A lifelong inveterate inventor who enjoyed the fascination of making things work.

Matthew Townsend. His invention of a latch-needle revolutionised the textile trade but brought him no prosperity.

and the United States and was described by his Patent Attorney as the most creative thinker he had ever encountered. As recently as 1993 he was working on instrumentation to measure the causes and effects of long-range air pollution, a most relevant line of research for the present day.

One of the earliest inventions to have a significant effect on the developing textile industry in Leicester and elsewhere in the nineteenth century was the latch-needle. The knitting industry was based on the hand frame which had been invented by William Lee in 1589. Although relatively slow, this could produce stocking stitch fabric in varying widths. Using 'bearded' needles, the frame could also make both socks and stockings. Matthew Townsend's invention of the latch-needle in 1847 changed the industry dramatically by enabling faster and more productive circular knitting.

Townsend was born in Cropston in the heartland of the rural Leicestershire textile industry in 1817. His father was a framework knitter and by the age of ten he was working in the same trade. By the age of twenty he was in Leicester, manufacturing luxury items for the hosiery market including cravats, shawls and gloves. He owned two hosiery factories with a workforce of over 400 people.

Townsend's latch-needle design was based on an earlier device patented in 1806 in France which had not been developed into a successful product. Townsend improved on the design and patented his modifications. However, in 1857, mainly due to reckless business deals, Townsend declared himself bankrupt. He settled his debts by selling his possessions and started a new life in Massachusetts where he entered a partnership with a garment manufacturer, Charles Draper.

William Taylor. His inventions included dimpled golf balls and cinematic lenses. Another man who could not resist a technical and engineering challenge.

This enterprise failed because an American version of the latch-needle had been patented before Townsend's version. He was sued for patent infringement and his new company was auctioned off.

The precursor of the well-known Bostik brand in Leicester was the Boston Blacking Company in Ulverscroft Road. The business fed into the wider shoe industry, making polishing wax and other materials to treat leather shoes, including a 'rubber cement'.

The company was founded in 1899 in Massachusetts, and in 1929 was acquired by the American United Shoe Machinery Corporation which had trading links with the British United Shoe Machinery Company in Leicester. By the 1930s, it was operating as the B. B. Chemical Company, supplying adhesives to the car industry. It was said that every British car manufacturer used at least two of their products. The brand name 'Bostik' was adopted by 1935.

Blu Tack was an accidental by-product. It was an attempt to develop a new sealant using chalk powder, rubber and oil. It was created in 1969 but the name of the inventor is unknown. Originally, Blu Tack was white, but research suggested that parents feared their children could mistake it for chewing gum, so a blue colouring was added. By 2015, Bostik was manufacturing around 100 tonnes of Blu Tack every week. Worldwide sales of Bostik products reached €1.5 billion and the company was employing nearly 5,000 people in more than fifty countries.

In the nineteenth century, scientific principles were rarely applied to sport, but in 1905, the principles of aerodynamics were used to redesign golf balls. The design now used worldwide was created in Leicester by William Taylor at his factory in Sparkenhoe Street.

Taylor was born in London in 1865 and moved to Leicestershire in 1885. He was a creative thinker, an engineer and a restless genius. After a bout of ill health caused by over-work, his doctor prescribed exercise and fresh air and suggested he take up golf, but even on the golf course his mind continued to think and to enquire. Taylor realised that the flight of smooth golf balls was slowed by drag. Contrary to expectations, the smoother the ball, the less distance it travelled. Dimples on a golf ball created a thin turbulent layer of air that would cling to the ball's surface. This allowed the smoothly flowing air to follow the ball's surface to the back of the ball, so decreasing the amount of the wake.

Systematically, he did tests to find the surface formation that would give the best flight. He then developed a pattern of regularly spaced indentations over the entire surface and built machine tools to produce this new type of golf ball in quantity.

William Taylor and his brother Thomas Smithies Taylor had founded a lens-making company in Leicester in 1886. It was an ideal combination of skills, William being an engineer and Thomas, an optician. They were responsible for developing the world's highest-quality cinema lenses which helped to develop

Established in 1886, Taylor-Hobson is a distinguished and well-respected brand, and still a world leader in their field.

*Above left and above right*: The National Space Centre in Leicester is an important educational facility as well as a celebration of space exploration.

the film industry in the early twentieth century. A third brother, J. Ronald Taylor, opened a factory in New York to make lenses for the Kodak Eastman company.

Taylors made numerous breakthroughs in optical technology, improving the science of meteorology, enhancing the capabilities of cinematic cameras and projection equipment and constructing instruments to calibrate lenses. In 1939 it is said that Taylor Hobson supplied over 80 per cent of the world's lenses for film studios. William was elected into the Royal Society in 1935. He died in 1937.

Possibly the most exciting and far-reaching project to be based in Leicester began on 30 June 2019 when a ceremony attended by Chris Skidmore, Minister of State for Universities, Science, Research and Innovation, politicians, university leaders and business leaders at the launch event, including Leicester mayor Sir Peter Soulsby, and University of Leicester president and vice-chancellor Professor Nishan Canagarajah, launched the construction of Space Park Leicester.

The site is next to the National Space Centre, home of the UK Near Earth Object Information Centre, and near the Abbey Pumping Station, designed by Leicester architect Stockdale Harrison where four massive steam engines built by the Gimson company of Leicester are still in working order after 130 years.

Aerospace and technology companies including Hewlett Packard, Airbus and Amazon have been signed up. When fully operational, the park could contribute up to £750 million a year to the economy as a world-leading manufacturer of satellites and a centre for processing the data they provide.

Space Park Leicester is also aiming to build a commercial Low Cost Access to Space (LoCAS) satellite manufacturing facility. It will provide a support network for the UK launch services now being set up and enable new companies and entrepreneurs to enter the market.

The National Space Centre was designed by Sir Nicholas Grimshaw CBE, who also designed the Eden Project in Cornwall and London's Waterloo International railway station. It opened to the public in 2001. The tower is 42 metres (138 feet) tall and is said to be the only place to house upright space rockets indoors. They are accommodated in a semi-transparent tower which has become one of Leicester's most recognisable landmarks. The Centre has on display one of only three known Soyuz spacecraft in the West.

The University of Leicester has been involved in astronomy and space research since 1961, less than five years after the former university college was granted a Royal Charter to award its own degrees.

In 1984, geneticist Sir Alec Jeffreys observed in his laboratory at the university a scientific phenomenon that would have worldwide significance. Jeffreys says he had a 'eureka moment' when looking at the X-ray film image of a DNA experiment which unexpectedly showed both similarities and differences between the DNA of different members of his technician's family. Within thirty minutes he had realised the potential of DNA fingerprinting using variations in the genetic code to identify individuals. His discovery led him to develop genetic fingerprinting and DNA profiling now used worldwide in forensic science. Sir Alec became a freeman of the City of Leicester in 1992 and was knighted in 1994.

His DNA method was first used in 1985 when he was asked to help in an immigration case to confirm the identity of a British boy whose family was originally from Ghana. The case was resolved when the DNA results proved that the child was closely related to the other members of the family, and Jeffreys always remembers the relief he saw in the mother's face when she heard the results.

DNA fingerprinting was first used by police in identifying the killer of two teenagers, Lynda Mann and Dawn Ashworth, who had been murdered in in the Leicestershire village of Narborough in 1983 and 1986. Not only was the murderer identified and subsequently convicted, but a major miscarriage of justice was prevented because the technology proved that the initial prime suspect was innocent. In fact, Colin Pitchfork, who was later sentenced for the murders, originally avoided taking part in the voluntary testing of men in the area by paying a friend to take his place. His arrest followed from a conversation overheard on a works night out in the Clarendon Pub in Leicester.

*Above*: Bicycle manufacture in Leicester fostered many clubs for enthusiasts as well as technical innovations and cycling competitions.

*Below*: Ernest Gimson's father was an iron founder in Leicester. His company's machines were an essential part of the Industrial Revolution, especially in the boot and shoe trade.

As well as leading research into DNA profiling and space exploration, the University of Leicester is where the academic study of English Local History began with the work of William George Hoskins CBE FBA who founded the first university department of English Local History. His outstanding work was in the field of landscape history. Hoskins demonstrated the profound impact of human activity on the evolution of the English landscape in his pioneering book *The Making of the English Landscape*. His work has had lasting influence in the fields of local and landscape history and historical and environmental conservation.

Hoskins would be taken to places of historic interest by Frederick Attenborough in Attenborough's car. Hoskins' usual mode of transport was his bicycle. Some of the photographs used in Hoskins' books were taken by Attenborough.

# Leicester Makes It Worldwide

In the nineteenth century, Leicester clothed the world. The knitwear company Wolsey celebrates its place in history as the oldest existing textile company in the world. It began in 1744 with the work of Leicester hosier Henry Wood. His widow, Ann, continued the business and she was followed by their sons and grandsons. In 1840, Robert Walker, an experienced hosiery manager, joined them, and when the last member of the Wood family retired in 1842 the company became Robert Walker and Sons. It was Walker who steered the business from its cottage-industry roots to fully mechanised factory-based production. The Wolsey name was adopted in 1920. It comes from a statement contemporary with the death in Leicester in 1530 of Thomas Wolsey claiming that he was buried in woollen cloth made in the town.

*Above left and above right*: The original artwork for Wolsey Knitwear's future marketing bears little resemblance to the traditional image of Cardinal Thomas Wolsey.

Significant publicity was gained when Wolsey underwear was chosen by explorers Captain Scott and Roald Amundsen in 1911 for their race to reach the South Pole. Some years later, Wolsey underwear was supplied, in accordance with Sir Ernest Shackleton's specifications, for his Murmansk expedition. In 1927 the Prince of Wales, later Edward VIII, visited the Wolsey Building and was presented with a cashmere scarf and a hunting pullover.

Wolsey is still in Leicester and continues to produce knitwear. In the 1960s it became part of the Courtauld group and was taken over by Matalan in 2002.

Throughout its history, Wolsey's marketing imagery has revelled in fine design.

Another delightful advertisement for Wolsey menswear, perfectly capturing the fashions and styles of the period.

In 2011, the company was taken out of Matalan by its owners, the Hargreaves family, who revived the brand by opening a shop in London's Covent Garden. To celebrate 250 years of manufacture, they launched a commemorative menswear collection in 2015.

The name Walker is synonymous with two other major companies which began in Leicester and are still based in the city. Henry Walker was a pork butcher who moved to Leicester in the 1880s, taking over an established high street business. The immensely profitable business he founded was a result of food rationing at the end of the Second World War. Meat was still rationed, and Walker would frequently sell out by mid-morning, leaving unsatisfied customers and staff without work. Potatoes were not rationed, so Walker offered them, thinly sliced and fried, as a substitute for meat.

The first Walkers Crisps production line was in the empty upper storey of his Oxford Street factory. In those days the potatoes were sliced by hand and cooked in an ordinary fish and chip fryer. Walkers make ten million bags of crisps every day. It is the UK's largest grocery brand, and the Beaumont Leys manufacturing plant in Leicester is the world's largest crisp factory.

Walkers also produced sausages and pies. A Leicester tradition for many years was queuing outside their Cheapside shop on Christmas Eve to buy a pork pie. This part of the business was acquired by Samworth Brothers in 1986. Production outgrew the existing premises in Cobden Street and was transferred to a new factory and bakery in Beaumont Leys on the outskirts of the city, coincidentally near to Walkers Crisps. Sold under the Walkers name and under several UK retailers' own brands, over three million hot and cold pies are made each week.

Trevor Storer launched Pukka Pies in 1963. At the time of his death in 2013, the company's annual turnover was over £40 million.

Six miles along the Leicester Western Bypass is the headquarters of Pukka Pies, which sells a further sixty million meat pies each year. The company was founded in 1963 by Trevor Storer. He was born in Leicester in 1930, attended Alderman Newton's School and left school at the age of sixteen to work in the family bakery, founded by his grandfather in 1899. Storer spent his National Service as an instructor at the British Army's bakery school.

The firm was sold to Allied Bakeries and Storer joined them as a trainee manager. He wrote a book called *Bread Salesmanship*, which was used by Allied as a training manual. He left Allied Bakeries in 1963, and sold his prize possession, an Austin-Healey Sprite, to fund his own company. Storer sold 1,200 steak and kidney pies in the first week with a turnover in the first year of £12,000. Originally making his pies in his own home, he built the company up so that when he died in 2013 he left his wife and two sons a company with an annual turnover of £40 million.

Leicester had numerous medieval markets. Today's city centre market, the largest outdoor covered market in Europe, grew from an early Saturday market and has seen the rise and fall of many businesses in its 800-year history.

Although laid out as a public park in the nineteenth century, Abbey Park still has the remains of walls and structures from earlier times.

In 1979, Bill Adderley was a manager at the Woolworths store in Coalville in north-west Leicestershire. The management wanted him to relocate to Skegness, but Bill refused, and consequently left their employment. Whilst looking for a new job, he and his wife Jean rented a stall on Leicester Market selling reject curtains from Marks and Spencer.

Five years later, they opened their first 'permanent' shop in Leicester's Churchgate trading as Dunelm Mill. In 1988, their first major store opened in East Street, Leicester, and two years later, their first store on the scale of those now operating opened in Rotherham. Until 1999, the business was managed from a

Leicester's new indoor market, completed in 2014, makes use of space and light. It is part of a longer-term refurbishment project.

The former Indoor Market which was built in the early 1970s. Many will remember the all-pervading smells from the fish market on the lower floor.

shop in Loughborough, but a purpose-built headquarters was built at Watermead Business Park near Leicester. Dunelm Mills, now the Dunelm Group, floated on the London Stock Exchange in 2006. The company operates more than 160 stores across the UK as well as selling online.

In 1930, a young man of twenty-four years and his fiancée opened a small hardware shop in a Leicester suburb. He was James Kemsey Wilkinson, and his shop became the first Wilkinson Cash Store. In the first week of trading, the couple managed a turnover of £23.

Wilkinson was born in 1906 in the Handsworth area of Birmingham. JK, as he was to be known by family and friends, left home at sixteen after his father's death. He gained retail experience by working for the chemists Timothy Whites, which at the time sold hardware as well as pharmaceuticals, and then followed in his father's footsteps, working for an architectural ironmonger in Birmingham before moving to Leicester to be employed by the ironmonger Herbert Pochin. He came to Leicester when he heard that the city was one of the wealthiest places in Europe. JK parted company with Pochins because his ideas for new products were not taken up by the management. Instead, JK went into business himself.

Wilkinson's first shop in Charnwood Street had a wooden floor and a counter running the length of the building back to Occupation Road. Customers remember the building smelling of paraffin and firelighters. Tony Wilkinson, JK's son, still remembers those smells. He also recalls a hatch in the floor leading to cellars where his father kept the stock.

Cavendish House in Abbey Park was built from the ruins of Leicester Abbey after its Dissolution in 1538, and just eight years after Thomas Wolsey was buried there.

The original shop moved later to No. 159 Charnwood Street and remained there until the street was demolished in the early 1970s, by which time the company had twenty-eight stores with an annual turnover of £2.4million. In 1963, the first Wilkinson store outside Leicester was opened in Melton Mowbray. In the same year, the Wigston Magna shop was moved to increase its floor space. The company now has over 400 stores and a turnover close to £4million per week.

The backbone of the nineteenth-century economy in many Midland towns and cities was the textile industry. It needed other industries such as dying and machinery manufacture, and together they provided mass employment and acted as a catalyst for entrepreneurs who went on to apply their skills and knowledge to new businesses.

In Leicester, the foundation stone of the large St Margaret's Works of Nathaniel Corah and Sons was laid in 1865. Nathaniel began his manufacturing career as a framework knitter on a Leicestershire farm. St Margaret's was the first factory in Leicester to be built with integrated steam power.

Henry Curry was born in 1850 and became one of the army of young men who had the vital role of keeping Corah's steam engines working. Many of the

The River Soar and the later canal connects Leicester's earliest history with its industrial heyday. Here the factories overlook the medieval Abbey Meadows.

men and women who worked at Corah and the other factories by the side of the River Soar and the Grand Union Canal in Leicester lived in the densely populated area which took its name from Wharf Street and connected the town with the wharf. Either side of this highway was a maze of streets, lanes, and courts. It was a poor area where many families lived in poverty, but a redeeming feature of the presence of the giant Corah works was their enlightened policy of caring for their workforce and offering wages above those of other local companies.

Henry Curry married Constance Mitchell in March 1870 and they started a family. They were to have ten children, eight surviving to adulthood. Curry found it difficult to provide for his growing family solely from his wages at Corah and so took on additional work. Making use of his mechanical knowledge, he began making bicycles for the Leicester Tricycle Company. His skills and apparent managerial abilities enabled him to join the company. In the 1881 census, he describes his occupation as 'fitter, tricycle works', but he went on to a management position at a time when the company was pushing forward the design of bicycles in a growing and competitive market.

Curry was working on technical improvements as well as supplying a steady demand for the 'ordinary bicycle' or Penny Farthing, and he was still working shifts at Corah. Finally, in 1884, at the age of thirty-four years, he and Constance went into business as bicycle manufacturers. They set up business in their garden

Henry Curry's first and second shops were in Belgrave Gate and the Haymarket. This photograph is of his second shop taken shortly before demolition to make way for the Haymarket Centre.

Lawrence Wright became a phenomenally successful music publisher and composer of chart-topping popular songs. His career began on a market stall in Leicester.

shed at No. 44 Painter Street in the shadow of St Mark's Church. The road is now the entrance to Leicester College.

It was a hand-to-mouth operation. Curry needed payment for one bicycle to fund the purchase of parts to build the next one, and he was only completing one bicycle each week. It was at this stage that Henry's business skills came to the fore. The potential bicycle market was massive and growing, and Leicester was at the forefront of development.

Curry caught the spirit and dynamism of the moment and saw the potential to modernise the bicycle, which was becoming a popular form of utilitarian and recreational transport. He secured premises at No. 28 Painter Street where he had the space to produce up to twenty-five bicycles each week. At the same time, he brought his sons, James and Edwin, into the business. Henry, the younger son, joined later in 1896. He added the new pneumatic tyres to his products, which increased his sales ten-fold, and developed bicycles marketed for safety, just ahead of rival developers.

Just four years later, he had acquired enough capital to open his first shop at No. 271 Belgrave Gate. The move was influenced by the inconvenience of potential customers calling at his small factory. He moved to larger premises at No. 296 Belgrave Gate in 1900 and then to No. 287 Belgrave Gate. When the Leicester Haymarket Shopping Centre was built in 1972/73, a plaque was erected at the junction of Haymarket and the clock tower, commemorating Curry's first retail premises.

A new company was formed in 1897 called H. Curry and Sons. James, Edwin and Henry (junior) were made directors on equal footing with their father. The youngest son, Albert, was just ten years old but was also involved at his request. Net profits in the following two years rose to the equivalent today of more than £100,000. The business expanded further, acquiring premises in Halford Street and Rutland Street, and, in 1907, setting up a head office and wholesale warehouse in Belvoir Street in the town centre.

The Halford Street association involved co-operation with Frederick Rushbrooke, a businessman from Birmingham who had set up a bicycle manufacturing business in that street. This became the Halford Cycle Company Ltd, the forerunner of today's Halfords retail chain.

The expansion continued. A new factory in Marlow Road, Leicester, was incorporated into the business in 1914 and larger office premises in Stamford Street were purchased in 1916. Another factory was established in Linden Street in 1918. In the same year, Curry's went to the capital by setting up a head office in London, in the heart of the city. In less than twenty-five years, a one-man business in the garden shed of a Leicester slum had become a nationally recognised industrial player.

Henry Curry retired in 1909. He died in 1916. His four sons carried the business forward, opening stores across the East Midlands in Leicestershire, Nottinghamshire and Lincolnshire. After the First World War, the company began to broaden its product range. The company continued to sell bicycles and accessories, although it stopped manufacturing them in 1932. Henry Curry had

*Above left and above right*: Donaldson was (with Amos Sherriff and George White) one of the three leaders of the 1905 Leicester march of the unemployed, and in later life became a canon at Westminster Abbey.

A rare photograph of Henry Curry and his family. All his sons became partners in his company.

always purchased from companies that produced quality products, and these, such as Lucas (lamps) and Dunlop, were to become familiar household names. By 1927, they had acquired the Campion Cycle Company and were also making and selling a variety of electrical goods including wireless receivers and gramophones.

After many takeovers and changes in branding, Currys became DSG Retail PLC. In the United Kingdom and Ireland, the group began merging Currys stores with their PC World chain, opening their first merged 'megastore' in Fulham in 2009 with the name 'Currys PC World'.

In 1934, the Leicester Rubber Company changed its name to the John Bull Rubber Company and launched a heavy tread car tyre to add to its range of car and motorcycle tyres and accessories. Three years later, the company took on a new venture under the name of Metalastik, producing rubber to metal products. The John Bull Tyre Repair Kit was a familiar and essential product for millions of cyclists and could be bought from a trade counter through a side door at the company's factory in Evington Valley Road. Dunlop acquired the company in 1959.

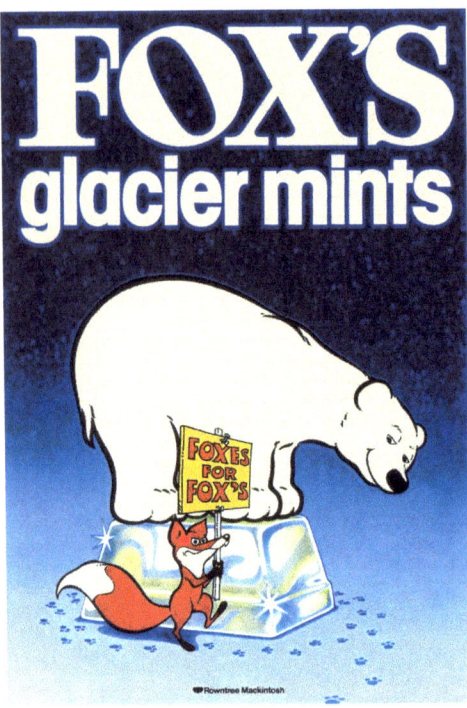

*Left*: Eric Fox created his famous glacier mints in 1918 and asked his workers to suggest a logo. The iconic polar bear image was developed by graduates of the Leicester School of Art.

*Opposite above*: William Everard's brewing business began as Hull & Everard in 1849. Steam-powered drays remained in use until 1946.

*Opposite below*: The Tower brewery. A dignified building designed by William Everard's nephew, John Breedon Everard. Water for the brewing process was drawn from springs located 300 feet below the building.

Fox's Glacier Mints were first made in Leicester in 1918. Eric Fox began producing confectionery in 1880. He held a staff competition to find a name and logo for the new product which led to the familiar Peppy the polar bear imagery, the work of Reginald Dalby, a graduate of the Leicester School of Art.

Beer has been brewed in Leicester since Roman times and several brewers were active by the nineteenth century including Jabez Penn, who built a brewery in Beaumanor Road in 1895. It was Everards that became the principal brewery. The company began as Hull and Everard in 1849 when William Everard, a farmer, and brewer Thomas Hull leased the Southgate Street Brewery from Wilmot and Co., the retiring proprietors. Although Hull continued as a maltster, Everard was the driving force behind the business, which he managed until his death in 1892.

The business expanded as the company progressively acquired outlets, with over 100 pubs by the late 1880s. In 1875, the company moved to a new state-of-the-art brewery designed by William's nephew, architect John Breedon Everard. On the corner of Southgate Street and Castle Street, it extracted pure water from wells 300 feet below the premises, and steam engines played a significant part in the mechanisation.

After William's death, the company passed to his son Thomas and brewing moved to Burton-upon-Trent which by the 1890s was producing 10% of Britain's beer. The Leicester Southgate brewery remained the distribution centre to the Leicestershire pubs with beer arriving by rail from Burton. The Trent brewery was purchased outright and renamed the Tiger Brewery.

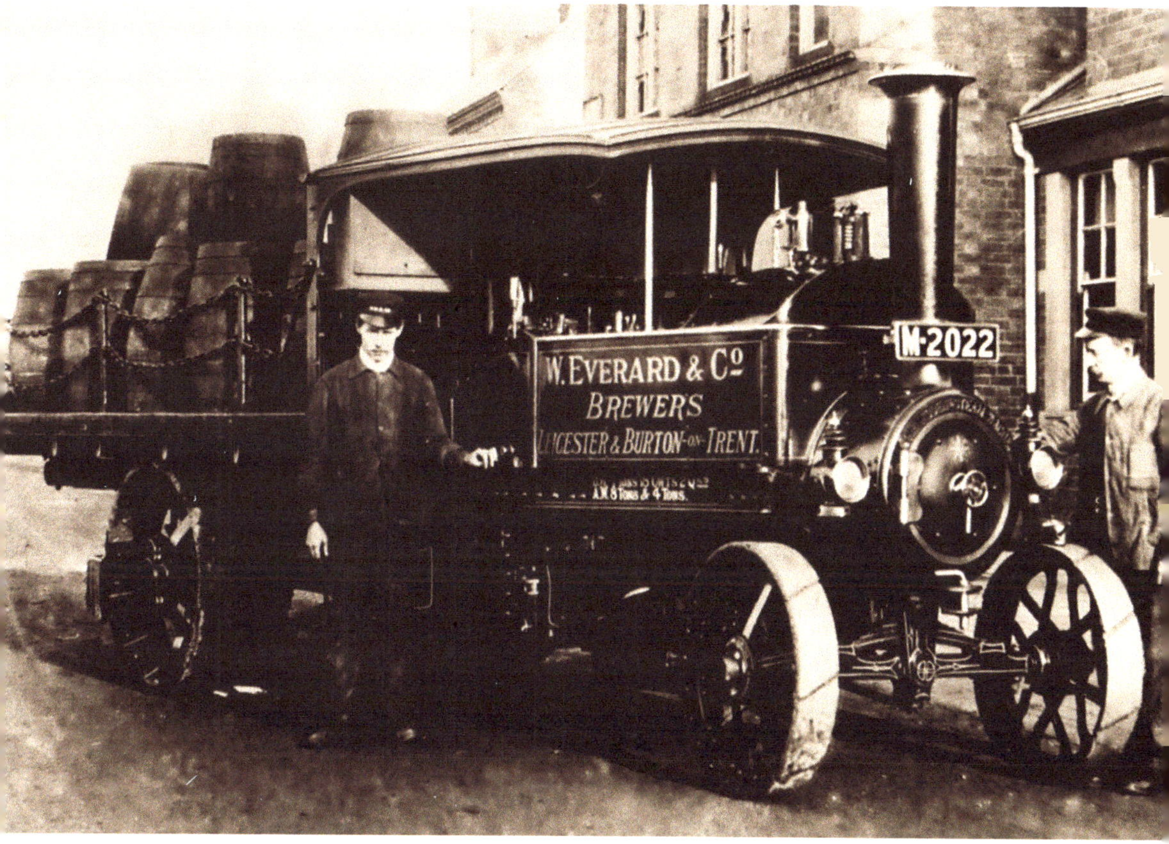
M-2022
W. EVERARD & Co
BREWERS
LEICESTER & BURTON-ON-TRENT

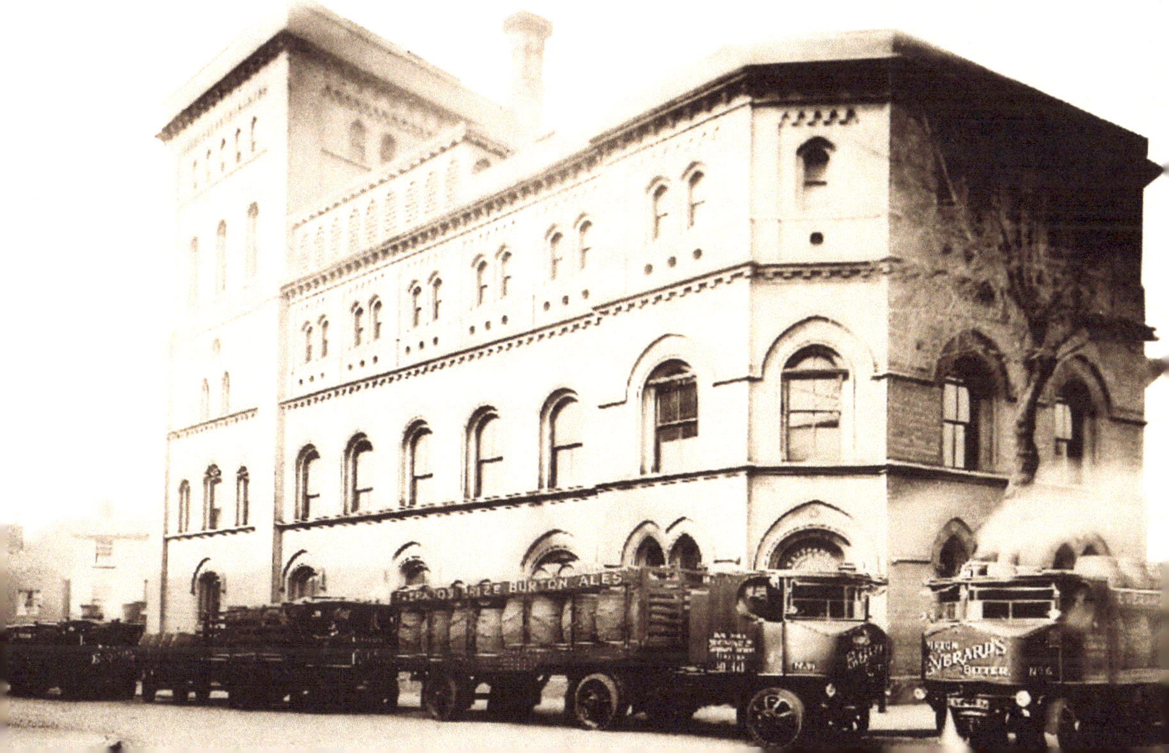
BURTON ALES
BITTER

Around 1920, Everards bought wine and spirit merchants John Sarsons and Son of Hotel Street, a major supplier to wealthy homes. Thomas moved his family to Nanpantan Hall. In 1921, a year which saw beer production peak at 55,000 barrels, the company acquired the Stamford Arms in Groby, the former home of his great-grandfather, and his grandfather, Richard Everard. Thomas died in 1925 and was succeeded by his son William Lindsay Everard.

The Great Depression saw a penny tax on beer. Production fell by a fifth and took five years to recover and all brewing ceased at Southgate in 1931.

Following Sir Lindsay's death in 1949, his son Tony Everard took over. He developed the concept of 'Friendly Inns' designed to 'look like your front room', which attracted women into what was traditionally a male preserve. Although pubs rarely came up for sale, the demolition of several older ones during construction of the Leicester inner ring road in the 1960s allowed the company to build new ones.

In June 2019, Everards began work on building a new brewery, beer hall and offices on a 70-acre site near Fosse Park. The development, called Everard Meadows, includes a cycle centre, café, a new pedestrian and cycle bridge across the River Soar and 2 miles of cycle ways. The Castle Acres site was sold to provide for extensions to the Fosse Park shopping centre.

*Liberty fashion shoes are the last word in footwear design and smartness, yet they give you an altogether amazing degree of comfort. That is the result of skilled craftsmanship in making. You look and feel better and smarter in Liberty shoes.*

**LIBERTY SHOES LTD., LEICESTER**

Influenced by a visit to New York, the Lennard family changed their company name to Liberty Shoes in 1921 and made great use of the image of the Statue of Liberty.

# Institutions, Charities and Sport

Leicester's first care home has been operating for nearly 700 years. Trinity Hospital, correctly titled the Hospital of the Honour of God and the Glorious Virgin and All Saints, was founded in 1330 by Henry Plantagenet, the Third Earl of Lancaster and Leicester, grandson of King Henry III and chief advisor to King Edward III.

The hospital was built to care for the poor and infirm and could accommodate fifty patients and staff including a warden, chaplains, and nurses. The first

The original hospital building was a long single-storey hall with a chapel at one end, divided by an arched aisle, so the services could be heard by all the residents in their rooms.

An earlier view of the frontage of Trinity Hospital before 1901, when one end of the building was rebuilt to make way for a new road.

hospital building was a long, single-storey hall divided by an arched aisle with a chapel at the end. The open design enabled all patients to see or hear services from their beds.

It was rebuilt in the late 1700s at the expense of King George III to create a two-storey building with rooms for staff, kitchens, washrooms and a sitting room. The tall pointed arches from this phase of building can still be seen around the entrance. The building underwent more changes in 1901 when increasing industry in the area required a new access to the town and a new bridge over the river. One end of the hospital was demolished and rebuilt at an angle. In 1994 the building was purchased by De Montfort University. The patients and staff were transferred to modern premises in Western Boulevard.

Behind the hospital is a garden which grew medicinal herbs for patients. This has been recreated in the style of an Elizabethan garden by the De Montfort

The herb garden at the rear of the former Trinity Hospital, now part of De Montfort University.

University Green Future Project to improve local biodiversity, providing cooking herbs and attracting wildlife to the campus.

In 2013, Leicester's other ancient care facility, the Wyggeston Hospital, celebrated its quincentenary, commemorating its founder, William Wyggeston, and celebrating its continued well-being as another caring institution for the twenty-first century.

William, a member of an influential family of wool merchants, prominent in the civic life of Leicester over several generations, founded his hospital in 1513. It was completed in 1518. It was licensed by King Henry VIII and funded by the income from Wyggeston's lordships, manors, and lands. In letters patent in 1572 it was decreed 'that the hospital should be for ever called "Wyggeston's Hospital", and that the Chancellor of the Duchy of Lancaster should appoint the Master and be a Visitor'.

St Martin's House was formerly the Wyggeston Hospital Boys' School which opened in 1877 on the site of the medieval Wyggeston Hospital. It was acquired by the Diocese of Leicester in 2008.

The Trustees also established a school for 200 boys and 100 girls between the ages of seven and seventeen. This formed the foundation of Wyggeston Grammar School for Boys and Wyggeston Grammar School for Girls. These are now co-educational sixth-form colleges, named Wyggeston and Queen Elizabeth I College and Regent College respectively. Wyggeston's Hospital makes an annual grant to the Trustees of the Wyggeston Schools Foundation which distributes this money with other income, making grants to students at the colleges.

A new hospital with a chapel dedicated to Saint Ursula was erected in 1868. The present hospital, built in 1966, occupies the same site and has fifty-four warden-assisted flats, all suitable for married couples.

It was the headmaster of the Wyggeston Boys' School who first campaigned for a university in Leicester. The Revd James Went repeatedly called for a University College to be set up, but no private funding was available, and the Corporation was already committed to the School of Art and the Technical School. In 1917, the *Leicester Daily Post* urged in an editorial that something more than memorials should be used to commemorate the dead. When the war ended, the local newspapers encouraged donations to form a university.

Thomas Fielding Johnson, a wealthy philanthropist who owned a worsted manufacturing business, purchased the old asylum building next to Victoria Park. He bought 37 acres of land for £40,000 and intended not only to house a college, but also the boys' and girls' grammar schools. Many donations, amounting to more than £100,000 were made in memory of loved ones lost during the war, and for those who had survived.

On 9 May 1921, Dr Robert Rattray was appointed Principal. Although only thirty-five, he was already a distinguished academic. Nine students enrolled to join the five staff when the college opened in October 1921.

In 1927, after it became a University College, students sat examinations for external degrees of the University of London. Two years later, it merged with the Vaughan Working Men's College, which had been providing adult education in

The original Wyggeston Hospital viewed from Peacock Lane. The hospital is now in modern premises and celebrated its 500th anniversary in 2013.

*Left*: Robert Fleming Rattray, the dynamic first principal of Leicester University. He led the then University College for eleven years and was succeeded by Frederick Attenborough.

*Below*: The Hawthorn Building, formerly the Leicester School of Art and now part of De Montfort University housing the faculties of Health and Life Sciences and Computing, Engineering and Media.

Leicester since 1862. In 1932, Dr Rattray was replaced Frederick Attenborough, who was the father of David and Richard Attenborough. In 1957, the University College was granted its Royal Charter and has since then had the status of a university with the right to award its own degrees.

In 2011, the university was selected as one of four sites for national high-performance computing facilities for theoretical astrophysics and particle physics. An investment of £12.32 million from the government's Large Facilities Capital Fund and investment from the Science and Technology Facilities Council and other universities contributed to the acquisition of a national supercomputer.

De Montfort University's origins lie in the Leicester School of Art which opened in 1870. The school responded to the changing needs of late nineteenth-century industry leading to the introduction of subjects such as engineering, building and machine drawing. By 1897, it was decided that the School's makeshift accommodation was no longer suitable. £25,000 was raised to build 'a very handsome school that would be enormous credit to the town and [...] so that it would answer its purpose for the next 100 years'. This was the Hawthorn Building in the Newarke which today still houses the sciences and the Faculty of Health and Life Sciences. At the time of the first phase of its construction, there were 500 art students and 1,000 technical students. Increasing demand for courses prompted an extension in 1909. In 1919, further properties nearby were rented. The Duchess of Atholl laid the foundation stone of Hawthorn's west wing in 1927, by which time the institution was renamed the Leicester Colleges of Art and Technology.

The Revd David Vaughan, from a family of dedicated philanthropists who contributed much to the well-being of the people of Leicester including the creation of Vaughan College.

Leicester Cathedral is the final resting place of King Richard III. The identification of his remains has been described as one of the top discoveries of the decade.

In 1966, the new Fletcher building was opened by Her Majesty, the Queen Mother, and a white paper, 'A Plan for Polytechnics and Other Colleges', was published, leading to the creation of the City of Leicester Polytechnic. This became De Montfort University in 1992, establishing it as a degree-awarding body in its own right. The name was taken from Simon de Montfort, the thirteenth-century Earl of Leicester who is credited with establishing, in 1265, the first English parliament. The university has around 27,000 full- and part-time students, 3,240 staff and an annual turnover in the region of £168 million.

Leicester Market has been a place of social and cultural importance since the thirteenth century when it became the centre for trade in the area. The first mention of it was in 1298 when 'a market took place bounded by the city walls and the corn wall'. The corn wall was a racetrack used by horse dealers to display the speed of their animals. The Domesday Book names the marketplace as 'Cheapside' from the Danish word 'chepe' meaning sell, a legacy of language left over from the Norse occupants of Leicester.

In 1589 Queen Elizabeth I mentioned the market in a charter, referring to it as the 'Saturday shambles'. A Wednesday market was also held at the High Cross (on Highcross Street) selling dairy, produce, vegetables and fruit. In 1884 the Wednesday market was moved to the same location as the 'Saturday shambles', which is where Leicester Market is today. Gradually the market became busier and by the 1850s it was held on Wednesdays, Fridays and Saturdays. It now operates six days a week, closing only on Sundays.

The Leicester Fosse team photographed in 1891, the year in which Filbert Street became their ground and when the club joined the Midland League.

The story of Leicester City Football Club's climb to the top of the Premier League reflects its 'rags to riches' move from the club's former ground at Filbert Street, its home since 1891, to the nearby King Power Stadium. Filbert Street changed little over the decades. Former manager Martin O'Neill joked that he led new signings out of the tunnel backwards, so they saw only the (relatively new) Carling Stand.

Plans for a new stadium were drawn up in 1998 but abandoned. A new plan was proposed in November 2000 for a 32,000-seat stadium near Freeman's Wharf on land next to Filbert Street. Work commenced in the summer of 2001 and the new stadium was completed on time, twelve months later. The opening was somewhat marred by Leicester City's relegation from the Premier League, which led to the club accruing debts of over £30 million. The stadium was opened officially by former Leicester striker Gary Lineker on 23 July 2002. Lineker used a giant pair of scissors to cut a ribbon on the pitch after arriving at the stadium in a Walkers Crisps lorry. It has a capacity of 32,313.

The first game at the new stadium was a friendly against Basque team Athletic Bilbao on 4 August 2002. The attendance was approximately 24,000. An exact

The Foxes Premier League success in 2016 prompted celebrations across the city. (Images courtesy of Victoria Lees, Annie Brookes & Steve Dovey)

figure could not be agreed because of a computer problem. The first competitive match took place six days later when Leicester beat Watford 2-0 in front of a near-capacity crowd of 31,022.

Leicester ended the season by gaining promotion back to the Premier League having lost just two home games and despite spending the early part of the season in receivership because of the huge debts.

In what was described as one of the greatest sporting stories of all time Leicester were confirmed as champions of the 2015–16 Premier League season on 2 May 2016, finishing top of England's highest league for the first time in the club's history. The club was 5000-1 with bookmakers to win the division before the season kicked off. Their success meant Leicester would be playing in the UEFA Champions League in the following season, a first for the club in their history. The season also saw history being made for individual players within the team. Jamie Vardy broke the record for goals scored in consecutive games in the Premier League (11) and Riyad Mahrez became the first African and first Algerian player to be the recipient of the PFA Players' Player of the Year award.

The longest-running women's football club in the league is Leicester Ladies FC. They celebrated their fiftieth anniversary in 2019.

Leicester Football Club was formed at a meeting on 3 August 1880 at Leicester's George Hotel which stood near the clock tower where the Haymarket Centre is now located. It was formed by the merger of three smaller teams: Leicester Societies AFC,

King Power Stadium opened in 2002 as the Walkers Stadium. It was renamed after the club's new owners in 2011.

Welford Road, the home ground of Leicester Tigers since September 1892. It is the largest purpose-built club rugby union ground in England.

Leicester Amateur FC and Leicester Alert. The new club's first game was a no-score draw on 23 October 1880 against Moseley at the Belgrave Road Cycle and Cricket Ground. In that first season they also played against Northampton, Nuneaton, Rushden, Market Harborough, Coventry, and Kettering among other clubs.

In 1881 the club joined the Midlands Counties Football Association, which meant they could enter the Midlands Counties Cup the following season. Tigers' first-ever cup game was an away loss to Edgbaston Crusaders. Tigers first appeared on television on 3 February 1951 in a match against London Scottish at the Richmond Athletic Ground. They won 14-0. Another milestone occurred on 18 November 1956, when, representing a city that was still traditional and conservative, the club played its first ever Sunday match. They lost to Old Belvedere in Dublin, 3-23. There were few innovations at the Welford Road ground during the 1950s, but in 1959, in tribute to the late Eric Thorneloe, who had served as Honorary Secretary between 1928 and 1957, clocks were installed on the stands. For most rugby supporters, the highlight of the year was the annual game against the Barbarians, a Boxing Day tradition that began back in 1909 and continued through to the end of the twentieth century.

In February 1998 Dean Richards was appointed Director of Rugby. Under Richards, Leicester entered a golden age, winning four consecutive Premiership Rugby titles as well as the Heineken Cups in 2001 and 2002. Tigers' third successive Premiership title came on 17 March 2001. That summer, Martin Johnson was named captain for the 2001 British and Irish Lions tour to Australia, becoming the first man to lead two tours. Leicester became the first side to retain a European title after beating Munster 15-9 in the 2002 Heineken Cup Final. Leicester also retained their fourth successive Premiership title in 2002.

Cricket came to Leicestershire in the early years of the eighteenth century from its birthplace in the southern counties of Kent, Sussex, and Surrey. The original 'laws of cricket' were written in 1744 and the earliest known reference to cricket in Leicestershire is a notice in the *Leicester Journal* of 17 August 1776 referring to the 'gentlemen cricketers of Barrow', namely Barrow-on-Soar. Framework knitters in towns and villages such as Barrow, Hathern, Long Whatton, Shepshed and

The Foxes premier league success in 2012 prompted civic-led celebrations across the city including Town Hall Square.

Loughborough, and in the south of the county, Hinckley, Lutterworth, Wigston and Fleckney, played the game because their hours of work were flexible enough to free up time in the afternoons to practice or play.

St Margaret's pasture near Abbey Park was the first regular home for cricket in Leicester and became the headquarters of many local clubs. The ground, now a multi-sports venue, is still an important part of the city's sporting and recreational activities. In 1825, the Wharf Street cricket ground opened, on a large site bounded by Humberstone Road, Wharf Street and Wheat Street. The Musician pub in Clyde Street stands on what was the outfield. The ground became nationally famous and was regarded by many as the finest ground in England, attracting many important matches.

However, the Wharf Street ground was sold for housing in 1860, and after a decade of uncertainty, cricket in Leicester moved in 1872 to Victoria Park, a racecourse which was adapted for cricket. A year later, W. G. Grace played there for the United South of England and in 1875 the first real county match for many years was played against Lancashire. Local clubs such as Ivanhoe, Banks, Leicester Town, South End, Temperance, Lansdowne, Dan Garner's, Oxford, Roslyn and St Mary's also played there. The County Club was created in 1820 and reformed in 1879 to become the Leicestershire County Cricket Club we know today.

Founded in 1967 and then known as the Loughborough All Stars, Leicester Riders is the oldest club in British basketball. Founder members of the National Basketball League in 1972 and the British Basketball League in 1987, the club moved from Loughborough to Leicester in 1981 with support from Leicester City Council and Leicester City Bus – hence the nickname 'Riders'.

The £4.8 million Morningside Arena, owned by the Leicester Riders Foundation, was officially opened in January 2016. It is used as the home venue for the team and for the Cobras, Leicester's wheelchair basketball team.

# Buildings and Special Places

The purpose of Leicester's oldest standing structure, the largest Roman remains outside London, was not understood until excavations by the pioneering archaeologist Kathleen Kenyon between 1936 and 1939. The remains were taken into state care in 1920 but largely disregarded until more extensive remains were discovered when a factory on the site was demolished. Some antiquarian historians had seen the Jewry Wall as a Roman or British temple possibly dedicated to Janus. Others identified it as part of a baths complex. In the nineteenth century it was regarded as one of the town's gates or as part of the town basilica.

Leicester's Roman baths were excavated over four seasons between 1936 and 1939 by Kathleen Kenyon.

Kenyon first believed that the site was part of the Roman forum. She later changed her opinion, suggesting that the earlier forum had been rebuilt as baths. Not until much later was the forum site confirmed as being to the east near to Jubilee Square. The Jewry Wall was then seen as the wall of a gymnasium which would have been part of the baths complex, but this is not accepted by all.

The name of the wall is also a mystery. It was known by its present name as early as the seventeenth century. One theory is that it relates to Leicester's medieval Jewish community which was expelled from the town in 1231 by Simon de Montfort. Another suggestion is that it is connected to the *jurats* of early medieval Leicester who formed the senior 'cabinet' of the Corporation and met in the town churchyard, possibly that of St Nicholas. The word is from the same root as 'juror', being someone who has taken an oath to perform a certain duty of judgment. The antiquarian William Stukeley used this name and accepted this definition for his map of Leicester published in 1772. It is now generally agreed that 'Jewry' represents a broader folk belief across Europe that tended to attribute the origin of any mysterious structure to the Jewish people.

The idea of a structure in honour of Janus has echoes in the Arch of Remembrance in Leicester's Victoria Park which is regarded by many as the finest structure of its kind in the United Kingdom. It was designed by Sir Edwin Lutyens after a commission in 1919 from Leicester City Council's Memorial

The Arch of Remembrance in Leicester's Victoria Park was designed by Sir Edwin Lutyens and constructed between 1923 and 1925.

Committee. It was originally intended that it would be built in Town Hall Square. Dr Douglas Cawthorne of the School of Architecture at De Montfort University has shown that Lutyens gave a specific solar alignment to the structure which can be appreciated only at sunrise on 11 November.

The work of another celebrated architect is at the heart of one of Leicester's largest post-war housing estates. The Parish Church of St Aidan was built by Sir Basil Spence. The foundation stone was laid in 1958, two years after work began on the new Coventry Cathedral, Spence's more famous religious building. St Aidan's was completed 1959. At the front of the church facing New Parks Boulevard is a large mural depicting the life of St Aidan, regarded as one of the best-surviving tiled murals of the post-war period. It was the first major tile commission of William Gordon who had previously produced studio pottery for the Walton Pottery in Chesterfield, Derbyshire. Spence's skeletal

*Above left, above right and right*: Three views of St Aidan's Parish Church in New Parks. The architect was Sir Basil Spence. The unique tiled mural is by William Gordon.

concrete bell tower is one of the most significant architectural elements of this building. A comparison has been made by some visitors with the tower of the nearby fire station.

Westbridge Place was originally known as the West Bridge Mill because of its proximity to the ancient West Bridge river crossing. This Grade II listed building was designed by local architect William Flint in 1844 for Whitmore and Sons who were worsted spinners. Five stories in height, it was built to dominate the local skyline and to demonstrate the economic power and dominance of the textile industry in Leicester. It has a grand slate pitched roof, an Italianate bell tower with three arched openings, and an ornate weathervane.

Whitmores became a branch of Paton and Baldwin's Limited and was known under that name until 1936. In 1949 H.T.H. Peck, known later as Pex, acquired part of the building but shared the site with Paton and Baldwin's and with the Leicester College of Art. It was still used as a worsted-spinning mill but later as a factory manufacturing socks and tights, particularly after the entire building passed to Pex in the early 1970s. In 1979, a fire gutted the front parts of the building. Eighteen fire appliances attended the blaze which could be seen from many areas of the city.

The building was refurbished in the 1990s when the glass extensions and front lift shaft were added. In 1994 Leicester City challenge made this building the

Westbridge Mill in its refurbished glory, having survived a major fire in 1979 and major rebuilding in the 1990s.

West Bridge Mill in its heyday, an example of the former might of Leicester's textile industry.

centre of regeneration for the area. Architects HLM and Loughborough-based builders William Davis Ltd were able to integrate the building into earlier work along the canal. The glass extensions on the front and rear were designed to reveal the original building and to provide extra space and light. The outside of the building is intended to have the appearance of a steam liner when viewed from the bridge. The cost of the refurbishment was in the region of £4.25 million pounds. Only Friars Mill and Westbridge Place remain of the twenty-six mills listed in the Leicester directory of 1826.

Known locally for many years as the Donisthorpe Mill, Friars Mill is Leicester's oldest surviving factory building. As the city's dominance in textile manufacturing developed, many of Leicester's finest factory buildings were constructed in this area around Bath Lane. The architectural historian Nikolaus Pevsner described Friars Mill as 'a brick building of seven bays and three storeys, with a three-bay pediment and a pretty clock turret, still entirely Georgian in style'.

The building closed in 2005 and suffered several years of neglect which led to decay and further damage. In 2012, it was severely damaged by fire. The building was purchased by Leicester City Council for £550,000 and a rebuilding and refurbishment plan began, costing £6.3million including £3.9million of European funding.

The completion of the project, including the former Pump House and adjacent Bath Lane Mill, was marked by the return of the factory's distinctive cupola. At the top is a decorative ibex which has been handcrafted to reflect the factory's original weathervane. The mill's new chimney has been refabricated in zinc and features bold Friars Mill lettering which is illuminated at night. The buildings provide accommodation for fifteen small- to medium-sized businesses and is a catalyst for the regeneration of the waterside area north of West Bridge.

Donisthorpe and Company was founded in 1739 but the name of the mill stems from the Black Friars of the Order of St Dominic who occupied the land beside the River Soar from around 1220. The earliest records of the company date to 1866 when Alfred Russell Donisthorpe was spinning yarn on the premises. In the twentieth century, the company narrowed its market and by the 1930s, F. W. Woolworth was the only company it supplied. Donisthorpes were taken over by the French company DMC in 1988 and in 2001 became part of the Amaan group.

It is only a short distance from the centre of the city, but Abbey Park seems a world away from the bustle of modern life. Like many municipal parks, it was a Victorian creation, but the land has a longer history reaching back to 1143 when Robert de Bossu, Second Earl of Leicester, founded, in the Augustinian tradition, the Abbey of St Mary de Pratis, dedicated to the Assumption of the Virgin Mary.

It was here that one of Leicester's most important historical accounts was written, by the librarian of the abbey, Henry of Knighton. He wrote of contemporary events between 1377 and 1395 as well as providing a historical record of the period between 1066 and 1366. Knighton offered a favourable account of John of Gaunt and describes the impact of John Wycliffe, who under Gaunt's patronage

Friars Mill, which, with West Bridge Mill, are the only mills out of twenty-six in the 1826 Leicester Directory to have survived.

and protection became rector of Lutterworth. Knighton also provided important material about how the Black Death affected the town including the impact on the price of food, grain and wine, wages and the availability of labour, and the sad statistic that almost one-third of the inhabitants of Leicester died of the Plague which struck in 1348/9.

At the Dissolution, the abbey and its lands were granted to the Marquess of Northampton who later sold both to William Cavendish, the First Earl of Devonshire. He built a substantial house using stone from the ruins. During the Civil Wars, the house was occupied by Royalist troops under Charles I and was deliberately gutted and set on fire after their departure. The charred ruins can be seen today.

The abbey ruins contain a memorial to Cardinal Thomas Wolsey, who was buried in the grounds. He died in Leicester on the way from York to London on 29 November 1530. A statue stands near to the park's café by the local nineteenth-century stonemason Joseph Morcom.

Close to the city centre, Abbey Park provides fresh air, a space for exercise and recreation, and beautiful landscaping.

Little remains of the abbey today, but its approximate 'footprint' is marked within the grounds. In recent years, much more knowledge of the abbey has been gained from archaeological surveys which have involved students at University of Leicester.

Plans to convert the 57 acres into a public park began in 1879 when the Corporation commenced wider flood-alleviation work along the whole stretch of the River Soar in the town. The work involved widening and deepening the river for a length of 1 mile, the excavated soil being used to landscape the parkland with mounds. Stone weirs and locks, and three new bridges were also constructed, more than 33,000 new trees were planted, and an artificial lake was created. It was opened by the Prince and Princess of Wales on 29 May 1882 and extended in 1932, the year of the great Leicester Pageant for which the park acted as an amphitheatre.

The park has been the venue for many major public events. An annual flower shower developed into the larger City of Leicester Show which ran from the 1940s until 1980s. Sections of the original abbey boundary walls have survived, bordering the modern St Margaret's Way. A small section of the same wall was repaired at some stage using stone retrieved from the Greyfriars church.

John Flower's lithograph of the ruins of Leicester Abbey in Abbey Park published in 1826. The ruins of Cavendish House (right) are still a familiar landmark.

The Abbey Pumping Station, now a museum, is a celebration of Victorian water engineering which brought sanitation and improved health to many. The four Gimson beam engines are all in working order.

For some years, as was the case with many municipal parks, Abbey Park suffered from lack of investment. Greenhouses fell into disrepair and the ornate flower borders were grassed over. Today there is a new interest in our green open spaces which are now regarded as important amenities. Abbey Park is once again in good condition and well-maintained. It is a valuable asset to the city and appreciated by hundreds of residents and visitors every day.

The Abbey Pumping Station is a fine example of decorated Victorian Gothic, with architectural features deserving of a grand city church. It was completed in 1891 to pump the town's sewerage to the then open fields at Beaumont Leys.

The building was designed by Leicester's Stockdale Harrison. Inside are four massive compound beam engines designed by Arthur Woolf and built by the Gimson Company of Leicester. All four engines have been restored to full working order. They are maintained by experienced and skilled volunteers from the Leicester Museums Technology Association. When installed, these engines pumped 208,000 gallons of sewage every hour. This is the only engine house in the world where four working examples of the same beam engine can be seen together.

The building was a major improvement to the town's sanitary arrangements. Until then, railway wagons and canal barges were used to move the waste from open sewers. The solution at the time was to pump all the waste from the town to 'farms' in the open countryside. The station operated until 1964 when electric pumps were installed and, soon after, a modern sewerage treatment plant was built at Wanlip, north of the city. The pumping station opened as a museum in 1972.

The Leicester architectural practice founded by Stockdale Harrison provided a legacy of fine buildings which still influence the urban landscape of the city. One of their most successful buildings, designed by Shirley Harrison, son of the founder of the practice, is the De Montfort Hall which was built in 1913. On land on the former South Field of the town, standing at the southern end of New Walk and near to Victoria Park and the campus of University of Leicester, the De Montfort Hall is dignified yet modest in scale and its Classical Greek style gives it a timeless quality. At its centenary in 2013 the building looked as smart and as appropriate to the surroundings as it does in photographs taken at its completion.

A simple reason why the hall looks impressive without being aggressively dominating is because of the open green space surrounding it. No buildings encroach, which allows the hall to be seen within a frame of green. Compare this setting with other civic buildings in Leicester, except for the Town Hall which has its square. Leicester's old Victorian theatres, and even its modern ones – the Haymarket and Curve – were designed to work within the confines of the urban environment.

The open setting gave the hall further benefits. There is an open-air amphitheatre on one side, almost hidden from view and sheltered from the worst of the elements by the hall. The space merges comfortably with the adjacent parkland and the campus of the university, giving visitors a sense of one garden, rather than several separate structures. The space prompted the hall to stage the successful 'Summer Sundae' outdoor festival for several years. Furthermore, Harrison's decision to leave space available for extensions to his original design has enabled a modest addition to be built on the Regent Road side.

The hall has accommodated a truly diverse range of events from school orchestras to wrestling, rock concerts to religious rallies. As well as a venue for artists of national and international distinction, it is where many young people from Leicester first performed in public. In the 1950s, a generation of young musicians with the pioneering County Music Advisor, Eric Pinkett, formed an orchestra which often performed at the hall, and fostered many other music ensembles and bands. In April 1953, over four days, more than 1,200 children from 120 Leicestershire schools sang and played on stage in the Leicestershire Schools Coronation Festival.

*Above and below*: These two photographs of the De Montfort Hall, taken ninety years apart, show how timeless the design is, the work of local architect Shirley Harrison.

*Above left*: Leicester's Guildhall was built by the Guild of Corpus Christi. It was Leicester's first town hall and accommodated the town's first police station. It is now a museum and a venue for wedding receptions and music and arts performances.

*Above right*: The Engineering Building at Leicester University, now a listed building, designed by James Stirling, and completed in 1963.

Leicester's first civic hall was the Guildhall. The first section was built in around 1390 as the meeting place of the Guild of Corpus Christi, a group of businessmen and gentry with religious associations and which had been founded in 1343. The building also accommodated a chantry priest who would pray for the souls of guild members in the adjacent St Martin's Church.

Many members of the Guild were part of the civic leadership of the town, and gradually the two roles overlapped. By the end of the fifteenth century, the Town Council was holding all its meetings in the Guildhall, and when the Dissolution of the Chantries Act came in 1563, the council purchased the building to use as its Town Hall. The Guildhall became the first police station in Leicester in 1836 after the Leicester Borough Force had been set up in the previous year. The building also houses the third oldest public library in England, established in 1632 in the east wing of the building. The books include a New Testament in Greek from the fifteenth century.

The fabric of the building, with its several wings, staircases and balconies, reflect the different periods in its history and the activities that were carried on here. These include the construction of quarters for the Chief Constable in 1840, later used as cells.

The BBC studios at No. 9 St Nicholas Place were built by the Leicester firm of Pick Everard in 2005 next to the medieval Guildhall.

By the beginning of the twentieth century, the Guildhall had fallen into disrepair. Its demolition was proposed, but after the intervention of the Leicestershire Archaeological and Historical Society, restoration work began, finishing in 1926 when the building opened as a museum. It is also said to be the city's most haunted building with no less than five ghosts! Today, the Guildhall houses the medieval Leicester Galleries, and it was here in the Great Hall that the formal announcement was given to the world's media that the remains discovered beneath the nearby Greyfriars car park were those of Richard III.

The Newarke or Magazine Gateway is still an imposing structure despite being surrounded by taller modern buildings. It was constructed in around 1400 as the main entrance to the Newarke precinct and was designed to impress rather than to have a defensive role. The exterior was heavily restored in the nineteenth century. It acquired the name Magazine Gateway after the Civil War when it was used for the storage of the town's weapons and gunpowder. The military association continued with the construction of Territorial Army barracks on part of what is now Magazine Square. In the twentieth century it also housed a museum collection dedicated to the history of the Leicestershire Regiment. This closed in the 1990s because the ancient staircase was unsafe.

Leicester's Central Ring road system was originally laid out either side of the Gateway, leaving it stranded between lanes of traffic and accessible only by

*Above*: The De Montfort University Students Union building in the Newarke which includes cafés and shops.

*Below*: The Newarke Gateway and Magazine Square in late Edwardian times. A sedate atmosphere, not reminiscent of the notorious 'whipping toms' activities of the past.

subways and steps. The road was later re-routed and the Newarke subway filled in. In 2012, Queen Elizabeth II became the first monarch for many centuries to pass through the gateway when she visited De Montfort University during her jubilee year.

The Stirling Building is complemented by the Attenborough (1970) and Charles Wilson (1966) buildings on the Leicester University campus, seen here at sunset across Victoria Park.

Although the architectural styles are somewhat confused, the quiet ambience of St Martin's Square, home to many independent retail shops, works well in the context of the old town.

# Traditions

There are many traditions that are special to Leicester. The delightful tradition of queuing to buy handmade pork pies in Cheapside on Christmas Eve is one that generations of Leicester people fondly remember. Traditions reinforce belief and make our communities and relationships stronger. They bring a sense of belonging and longevity.

The Whipping Toms was a tradition carried out each year on Shrove Tuesday in the Newarke, land next to the castle which for centuries was outside the jurisdiction of the town. The first occurrence of the event is unknown, but the earliest recorded mention is in 1744.

The day would begin with a fair in the Newarke which included music, food, drink and entertainment. The mood was festive with people gathering from across Leicester to celebrate. A hockey-like game was played, with the gates to the Newarke being used as goals. The game would end soon after midday, with most women and young children vacating the area at this time.

At 1.00 p.m., three men wearing blue smocks and armed with a large wagon whip appeared, attended by three other men, one of whom carried a bell. These were the Whipping Toms, who claimed the right of flogging any person they could catch. The men and boys who had remained would surround the bellmen and try to capture his bell, running the risk of a severe whipping by doing so.

The custom was a celebration of the expulsion of the Danes from Leicester in the tenth century but was also an excuse for casual violence fuelled by alcohol. Fighting would often break out. The tradition was banned by the Leicester Improvement Act, passed by Parliament on 16 February 1846.

One ancient tradition, held on the Feast of St John the Baptist, still takes place each year at a pub in Loseby Lane, and it has associations with the Newarke. The Lord Mayor of Leicester with members of the Guild of Freemen of the City of Leicester, collect a Damask rose as the annual peppercorn rent.

Elements of this quaint ceremony date to medieval times as in the choice of a red rose, the emblem of the House of Lancaster. The pub stands near a parcel of land formerly owned by the Honour of Lancaster. Some historians believe it may have been the site of a hostel of the College of St Mary of the Annunciation in

The old and the new. Looking towards Magazine Square, the tower of St Mary de Castro, now without its spire, seen between the Hugh Aston Building of De Montfort University and the medieval Newarke Gateway.

the Newarke, established in 1361. The church within the college was built as a mausoleum for members of the House of Lancaster – hence the choice of a deep-red rose, the emblem of Lancaster.

After the Reformation, the college was closed, and its land and holdings sold off. On 24 February 1636, the land in Loseby Lane, next to his own property, was purchased from the Duchy of Lancaster by a local shoemaker, James Teale, and Elizabeth, his wife, for two pounds on condition that they also paid an annual peppercorn ground rent of four pennies and a deep-red Damask rose on the Feast Day of St John the Baptist. The record of the contract has survived, and states:

> To beholden of our said sovereign lord the King his heirs and successors as of his honor of Leicester in the right of his Highness, Duchy of Lancaster by fealtye only in common soccage and not in Capital: Yielding and paying therefore yearly unto the mayor of the Borough of Leicester for the time being one Damask rose at or upon the feast day of Saint John the Baptist

Sometime later, a public house was built on the site. By 1729, it is noted in the Records of the Borough of Leicester as the Red Cow, the landlord being Samuel Coates. In an entry for 1771, the payment was recorded as being made by 'the heirs of Executors of Samuel Coates for a house later called the *Star and Ball* and now the *Crown and Thistle*, late the land of Jackson in the occupation of Alexander Forrester'. The date is given as Midsummer, also St John's Day, one of England's quarter days when rents were due.

The tradition continued until the end of the twentieth century while Ind Coope owned the pub and when the rent was collected by the City Treasurer, but then fell into abeyance until 2010 when the Lord Mayor, Councillor Colin Hall, restored the tradition by calling to collect the rent in his formal robes and chain of office. A plaque has been installed on the premises explaining the ancient custom for the benefit of visitors.

There are other fascinating stories about this building, including a claim that a tunnel exists connecting the pub's cellars to the cathedral, and that it was an overnight resting place for Lady Jane Grey.

A powerful Leicester legend is that of Black Annis. She is said to be the witch who confronted King Richard III on his way to the Battle of Bosworth on 22 August 1485. As he led his army out of Leicester, his spurs struck a stone pillar on Leicester's Bow Bridge and the witch leapt out, declaring that it would be his head that would collide with the same obstacle on his return.

Marking the boundary of the castle precincts and the Newarke is the Turret or Prince Rupert's Gateway where Black Annis is said to menace passers-by at midnight.

According to legend, Black Annis used her iron claws to dig into the side of a sandstone cliff, west of the town of Leicester, to make herself a home which became known as Black Annis's Bower. In front of the cave was a large oak tree in which she would hide so that she could leap out and grab lambs and young children who had wandered too far from home. She would drink their blood, eat their flesh and hang their skins up in her cave to dry. Some traditions say she wore a skirt sewn from the skins of her human prey.

Her bower was a cave in the Dane Hills area, now Newfoundpool, Western Park and New Parks. Until just after the First World War, a cave still existed on a small natural outcrop on the Dane Hills, west of the city towards Glenfield, which was believed by many as her lair. By the late nineteenth century it had been filled in. An eyewitness of that time described its dimensions as around 4–5 feet wide and 7–8 feet long, 'having a ledge of rock, for a seat, running along each side'. It is now beneath the Dane Mills housing estate which covers the area in the square of land bounded by the A50 Groby Road, A47 Hinckley Road, New Parks Way and Tudor Road.

A secret tunnel was said to connect Black Annis' home to the castle in Leicester. It is said she also haunts the gateway of the castle and the Turret Gateway along the path to the Newarke, moving along her secret underground tunnel from the Dane Hills, and sleeping in the castle cellars.

*Reordering a churchyard can be controversial, but the project here has created a respectful open space connecting the cathedral to the Greyfriars area where Richard III's remains were discovered.*

The Christian perspective of good and evil is reflected in a more recent and now well-established tradition. 'Christ in the Centre' is a dramatic recreation of Christ's passion, trial, crucifixion and resurrection. It has been staged in Leicester's city centre nearly every year since 2003 and is one of the longest-running events of its kind in the country, attracting over 10,000 spectators.

Despite racial unrest and tensions in other cities, Leicester has a long history of religious and racial tolerance. The city has been home to men and women from all walks of life who have led a remarkable range of different movements giving working-class people a voice. These have included Christian Socialism represented by Revd Frederic Donaldson, trade unions, the Co-operative movement, and the influential Great Meeting whose members dominated the city's political leadership for decades. All have played their part in creating a cultural, political and religious environment of great strength and unity.

Another reason for Leicester's standing as a city where numerous cultures can live together peacefully is its ancient geographical location, being on the southern edge of the Danelaw, where Danish customs and law held sway for centuries, and Mercia, the Saxon kingdom which dominated England for 300 years. Mercia derives from *merce* in the West Saxon dialect, meaning border people. Leicester was a meeting place where different cultures and influences met and exchanged ideas as well as goods.

Leicester has more recently been described as a City of Festivals. Every major religion celebrates its traditions and beliefs by taking to the city's streets. The city has a rich social and cultural heritage of legends and customs that include religious ceremonies, decoration of homes and temples, time with family and friends, feasting and exchanging gifts.

Leicester's Diwali celebrations are some of the largest outside India, focused along the 'Golden Mile' of the Belgrave Road in the heart of the city's Asian community. The annual switch-on of the Diwali lights is in the form of a street party attended by 35,000 people, with dance, music and food to celebrate the Festival of Light.

The Newarke Bridge across the 1-mile straight of the canalised River Soar. Once an industrial landscape, it is now a pedestrian route connecting De Montfort University and the King Power Stadium to the town.

*Left*: The brightly coloured outfits for Leicester's annual Caribbean carnival take many months of careful work to design and create.

*Opposite above*: Leicester's Town Hall. A quiet and dignified building on the site of the town's former horse fair.

*Opposite below*: This crowd in Leicester Market is welcoming the return of those who had taken part in the march of the unemployed to London in June 1905.

Also celebrating the city's cultural diversity, the Leicester Caribbean Carnival, founded in 1985, is one of the biggest celebrations of Caribbean culture in the UK. The day starts with the carnival parade with numerous brightly – coloured floats featuring costumed bands and dancers making their way through the city. Festival goers then go to a carnival village in Victoria Park to share food, music, dancing and family entertainment.

The Leicester Comedy Festival boosts the local economy by more than £2million every year. In 2013, the festival involved over 500 events in more than fifty venues in Leicester and Leicestershire. It was the brainchild of Geoff Rowe when he was a student at Leicester Polytechnic. Bored, and finding little to do in his village, Geoff promoted his first concert at the age of thirteen in his village hall. It was successful and gave him the stimulus to arrange further events throughout his teenage years.

He worked briefly in the music industry in London before moving to Leicester to start an Arts Administration course at the former Scraptoft campus of De Montfort University. One of his student placements was the opportunity to be involved in the public celebrations for the opening of the Channel Tunnel in Folkestone.

As part of his final year studies Geoff helped launch the Leicester Comedy Festival in 1994. That first festival involved forty events in twenty-three venues over one week throughout Leicestershire. The acts included Matt Lucas and Harry Hill, and the events attracted over 5,000 visitors. Geoff was awarded the British Empire Medal for his services to comedy in the Queen's Jubilee Year and was given an honorary Doctor of Arts in 2012 from De Montfort University.

*Traditions* 87

# Music, Arts, and the Media

It is possible that Geoffrey Chaucer put pen to parchment in Leicester. He stayed in the town when visiting his patron, John of Gaunt. It is said that he and Philippa de Roet were married at St Mary de Castro. Philippa's sister, Katherine Swynford, was John of Gaunt's third wife. So, Leicester may have a writing tradition stretching back almost 700 years. Another popular story claims that in the sixteenth century Shakespeare came to Leicester's Guildhall with a company of actors, and that he first heard the tale of King Leir during that visit.

Playwright John Kingsley Orton's career was short but dramatic and controversial. Over three years from 1964 to 1967 he shocked, outraged and amused audiences with his black comedies. He was born at the Causeway Lane Maternity Hospital in Leicester. His father was a gardener for the Borough Council and his mother worked in a shoe factory. From 1966, the family lived on Leicester's Saffron Lane estate.

Orton went to Marriot Road Primary School and failed the eleven-plus because of illness. His first job was as a junior clerk working for £3.00 per week. He became interested in theatre in his teenage years, joining groups including the prestigious Leicester Dramatic Society. He took elocution lessons and body-building courses and was accepted for RADA (the Royal Academy of Dramatic Art) in 1950.

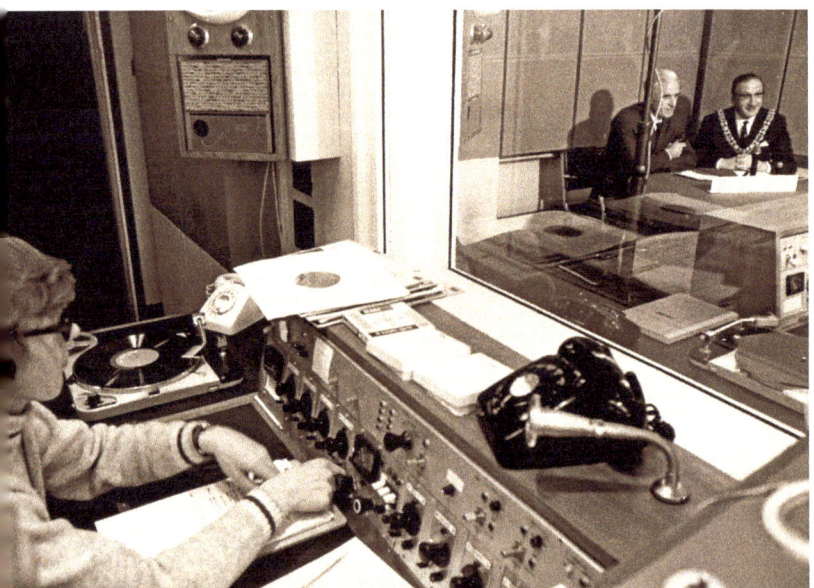

The Operations Room and Studio 1 at BBC Radio Leicester, the first local radio station on the English mainland. These photographs are from the opening day on 8 November 1967.

Orton's short but intense career ended on 9 August 1967 when he was murdered by his lover Kenneth Halliwell at his home in Islington. Halliwell committed suicide. Joe Orton was cremated at Golders Green Crematorium.

His legacy lives on in Leicester. The pedestrian concourse outside the main entrance to the Curve theatre is named Orton Square.

Colin Wilson was one of the most influential writers of his time. He was just twenty-four when *The Outsider*, his first major work, was published in 1956. It has never been out of print and has been translated into more than thirty languages.

Wilson also wrote about the occult and crime, including *Jack the ripper, Summing Up and Verdict*. He invented the term 'ripperologist'. He was prolific in both fiction and non-fiction and was still writing at the time of the illness which led to his death in 2013. On 1 July 2016 the First International Colin Wilson Conference took place at the University of Nottingham.

The daughter of a Leicester postman, Sue Townsend attended Glen Hills Primary School, South Wigston High School and Mary Linwood Comprehensive School. She left school at the age of fifteen and took a number of jobs in local factories and shops. By the age of twenty-two she was married with three children.

An early outside broadcast by BBC Radio Leicester from the Palais in Humberstone Gate.

It was not until Sue was in her thirties that she began writing with a group at Leicester's Phoenix Theatre, and by the time she wrote the first Adrian Mole novel she had moved to the Saffron Lane estate, coincidentally, near Joe Orton's former home.

Adrian Mole, for whom Sue drew upon personal experiences including her own schooldays and her son's childhood, brought her international fame, but she also wrote several plays and two non-fiction works including *Why Britain Needs Its Welfare State*, including themes she used in a series of superb commentaries on social issues for the *Observer* newspaper.

Franklyn Edmund Ward established a publishing company in Leicester to provide business for local printers Raithby Lawrence, also known as the De Montfort Press. Ward was a director of the firm. During the Second World War, he advertised in *The Times*, inviting manuscripts from new children's authors. The first publication, in 1943, was a book with colour illustrations titled *Rhymes for Young Nature Lovers*. Thirteen other titles were added before Edith Gregorson submitted the manuscript for three railway stories, written by Wilbert Awdry. Like most publishers of children's book of the time, Ward bought the copyright of the books for an outright fee instead of paying an advance and royalties. He bought the copyright of Awdry's stories for £25.

Initially intended to be published as separate books, Ward opted to publish them as one, and asked Awdry to write a fourth story to complete the work. He refused to commit to a publication date because wartime shortages made it

Don Kotak, a pioneer in local broadcasting for Leicester's Asian community. A photograph from the late 1960s.

The interior of St Mark's, Belgrave Gate. The Revd Frederick Donaldson, known as the 'vicar of the unemployed', commissioned dramatic socialist murals as backdrops to the altar. The church is now a banqueting centre.

difficult to acquire paper. Printing finally began in February 1945 with an initial print run of 22,500. The book was a massive success and two additional print runs of 17,000 and 16,000 were issued within months. In July 1945, Awdry submitted the manuscript for a second book, which was accepted for publication two months later.

Ward was also responsible for discovering several talented young illustrators, recruited from the Leicester School of Art. These included John Theodore Kenney and Clarence Reginald Dalby who were illustrators for the Thomas the Tank Engine books.

Leicester was the birthplace of Lawrence Wright, one of the world's greatest music publishers who wrote numerous popular songs under the pseudonym of Horatio Nichols. Wright first sold music scores from a stall on Leicester Market, later opening a shop in Conduit Street near the railway station in 1906. Shortly afterwards he wrote his first successful song, 'Down by the Stream'. By 1912 he had established the Lawrence Wright Music Company in London's Denmark Street. Wright wrote or co-wrote over 600 songs including the propaganda song of the First World War 'Are We Downhearted? No!'. In 1926, he launched the popular music journal *Melody Maker*.

Il Rondo in Silver Street. The biggest names in pop and rock music of the 1960s played here.

Many entertainers including musicians and singers have performed on the stage of Leicester's De Montfort Hall including those whose careers began here. Sir Michael Tippett, one of the greatest classical composers of the twentieth century, was 'turned on to music' as a schoolboy when he heard a performance at the De Montfort Hall by the Leicester Symphony Orchestra. At the time, he was a student at Stamford Grammar School where Malcolm Sargent taught music. Sargent, later to become the iconic conductor of the last night of the BBC Henry Wood Promenade concerts, was then the conductor of the Leicester Symphony Orchestra.

John (or Jon) Lord is known for his pioneering work in the fusion of musical genres. He grew up in Averil Road in Leicester and attended Wyggeston Boys' School. He studied classical organ and piano and became strongly influenced by blues music and artists such as Jerry Lee Lewis and Buddy Holly, whom he saw at the De Montfort Hall. With bands including Deep Purple, Whitesnake and even the Flower Pot Men, he explored the fusion of classical baroque and rock.

One of his many career landmarks was the 'Gemini Suite', commissioned by the BBC and performed by Deep Purple with the Light Music Society under Malcolm Arnold at the Royal Festival Hall in 1970, and later in Munich with the Kammerorchester conducted by Eberhard Schoener.

In 2010, he was inducted as an Honorary Fellow of Stevenson College in Edinburgh. In the following year he was awarded an honorary Doctor of Music degree at the De Montfort Hall by the University of Leicester. He was posthumously inducted into the Rock and Roll Hall of Fame in 2016 as a member of Deep Purple.

Other popular singers and musicians from Leicester include Engelbert Humperdinck, Roger Chapman of Family, John Deacon of Queen, Showaddywaddy and, most recently, Kasabian.

Of an earlier era, the Dallas Boys were an early boy band. They comprised of four former pupils of Moat Boys' School – Joe Smith, Stan Jones, Bob Wragg, and Leon Fisk – and London-born Nicky Clarke. After winning a Butlin's talent contest, they performed regularly on television shows including *The Six-Five Special*.

In the broadcast media, Leicester can claim several firsts. The BBC's first local radio station, BBC Radio Leicester, began broadcasting from studios on the eighth floor of Epic House, an office block in Charles Street, on 8 November 1967.

From the beginning the station recognised the increasingly diverse nature of Leicester, broadcasting a programme called *All Together Now* aimed at the immigrant communities in the city. This was followed by a weekly programme in Hindustani from 1972. Continued immigration to Leicester from East Africa, notably Kenya and Uganda, saw BBC Radio Leicester launch the first daily programme for Asian listeners in Britain. The *Six o'clock Show* combined news with music and entertainment and made an important contribution to social cohesion in the city. Research showed the programme to be hugely popular; two thirds of Asians in the city listened regularly and a further quarter listened occasionally.

Don Kotak, one of the original presenters of the *Six o'clock Show*, went on to present an Asian programme on commercial radio in the city. Born in Nairobi, he

The former Fosseway Pub, located as its name suggested, on the Fosse Way north of Leicester, is where two local bands, double-booked to play on the same night, joined forces to become Showaddywaddy.

came to England in 1966 and gained a degree from Leicester Polytechnic. Moving to Centre Radio in 1981, he launched a new Asian programme but ensured it did not clash with the BBC's show, so increasing the availability of Asian radio in the city. By 1989, SABRAS, meaning 'all tastes', was broadcasting on medium wave for four hours every night of the week.

With community support Don won the franchise in 1995 to launch SABRAS as a stand-alone twenty-four-hour Asian radio service in Leicester broadcasting from the former St Michael and All Angels church on Melton Road in Belgrave.

The *Six o'clock Show* on BBC Radio Leicester became a fledgling BBC Asian Network in 1989 and was later relaunched nationally from Leicester in 2002 as part of the BBC's digital radio network. Both SABRAS and the BBC Asian Network are still on air.

Leicester is also home to Takeover Radio, the UK's first independent radio station led by young people. Managed by the Takeover Radio Children's Media Trust, the station is run entirely by volunteers. During school time, the station is looked after by a team of volunteer adults who hand the airwaves back to young people in the evenings, at the weekends and during school holidays.

Takeover began as a single programme on Valley FM, a small community radio station in Market Harborough. It received its licence to broadcast full-time in 2001, and in 2010 moved to its present studios in one of the Victorian gatehouses at Leicester's Abbey Park. It is probably the only radio station in the UK to be based in a public park!

Many stars of the stage, the silver screen and television dramas began their careers in Leicester. Rakhee Thakrar, known to BBC *EastEnders* viewers as Shabnam Masood, has also starred as Emily Sands in the Netflix series *Sex Education*. In Leicester, she was a member of the cast of the groundbreaking radio

Biddy Baxter, the driving force behind *Blue Peter*, the longest-running children's television programme in the world. She became the programme's editor at the age of twenty-nine.

soap *Silver Street* on the BBC Asian Network and an influential member of the team running Hathi Productions, providing teenagers in Leicester the opportunity to work towards a career on stage.

Parminder Kaur Nagra was one of the first members of the Leicester Asian community to achieve international stardom. She is the eldest child of Sukha and Nashuter Nagra, Sikh factory workers who emigrated from the Punjab region of India in the 1960s. Parminder went to Northfield House Primary School and Soar Valley College, where she played viola in the youth orchestra and appeared in her first theatrical productions.

Soon after her A levels while working front-of-house at the Haymarket Theatre, her former drama instructor invited her to join Hathi Productions. She agreed and was cast as a chorus member in the 1994 musical *Nimai* presented at the Haymarket. One week into rehearsals, she replaced the lead actress.

Her international television and film careers have included the role of 'Jess' in *Bend it like Beckham* (2002), Dr Neela Rasgotra in the American television medical series *ER*, and Dr Lucy Banerjee in Fox TV's *Alcatraz*. She has had several other major television roles including starring as Meera Malik in the NBC crime drama series *The Blacklist* and a recurring role on the ABC/Marvel Television series *Agents of S.H.I.E.L.D.* as Ellen Nadeer.

Film director Stephen Frears was born in Leicester in 1941. His mother was a social worker and his father, a general practitioner and accountant. Frears has produced numerous landmark films in his distinguished career including *My Beautiful*

Curve, Leicester's impressive theatre in the heart of the city's cultural quarter, reflects the world outside as well as revealing to passers-by how modern theatre is made.

*Laundrette* (1985), *Prick Up Your Ears* (1987), *Sammy and Rosie Get Laid* (1987), *Dangerous Liaisons* (1988), *High Fidelity* (2000) and *Victoria & Abdul* (2017).

Michael Kitchen, now best known as Christopher Foyle in the ITV drama *Foyle's War*, was also born in Leicester. He was head chorister in the Church of the Martyrs choir where he was a regular soloist. He attended the City of Leicester Boys' Grammar School and once appeared on stage in a school production of *Cymbeline*.

First broadcast on 16 October 1958, *Blue Peter* had been devised by John Hunter Blair, but it was Biddy Baxter and her deputy Edward Barnes who developed the format into a successful programme, initially on a budget of just £180 per edition. When they were first introduced, Barnes was told, 'You'll have to look after Biddy – she doesn't know very much.'

In 1963, she devised and introduced the *Blue Peter* badge to encourage children to send in programme ideas, pictures, letters and stories, and she introduced the now famous annual appeals. She was awarded a gold badge herself when she retired. Having been disappointed as a child to receive the same reply twice to different letters she had written to Enid Blyton, Biddy introduced a card index system so *Blue Peter* viewers could receive more personal responses. She became programme editor in April 1965 following a reorganisation.

By some presenters she was seen as a divisive figure. Valerie Singleton has said Biddy treated the presenters like children, but Peter Purves has said, 'the programme succeeded – and I've said this many times – because of her, not in spite of her. She absolutely ruled it; I didn't always agree with her views, but she was right.'

In the 1981 New Year Honours, Biddy was awarded an MBE in recognition of her work. She is a fellow of the Royal Television Society and has honorary doctorates from Newcastle University and Durham University. In November 2013, she was the recipient of the Special Award at the BAFTA Children's Awards in 2013.

Dubbed Britain's first boy band, the Dallas Boys came not from the States, but from Leicester where they all attended Moat Boys' School, with the exception of London-born Nicky Clarke.